HUNTING WITH HARKER

HUNTING WITH HARKER

Peter Harker and Keith Eunson

A.H. & A.W. REED
WELLINGTON · SYDNEY · LONDON

First published 1976

A.H. & A.W. REED LTD

182 Wakefield Street, Wellington
53 Myoora Road, Terrey Hills, Sydney 2084
11 Southampton Row, London WC1B 5HA
also
16-18 Beresford Street, Auckland
165 Cashel Street, Christchurch

© 1976 PETER HARKER and KEITH EUNSON

All rights reserved. No part of this publication may be reproduced, stored in a retrieval system or transmitted in any form or by any means electronic, mechanical, photocopying, recording or otherwise without the prior written permission of the publishers.

ISBN 0 589 00950 8

Typeset by Joseph Churchward Ltd, Wellington.
Printed by Kyodo-Shing Loong Printing Industries
Pte Ltd Singapore.

To my Father . . .
A Good Keen Man who introduced
me to the pleasures of hunting
and the high country.

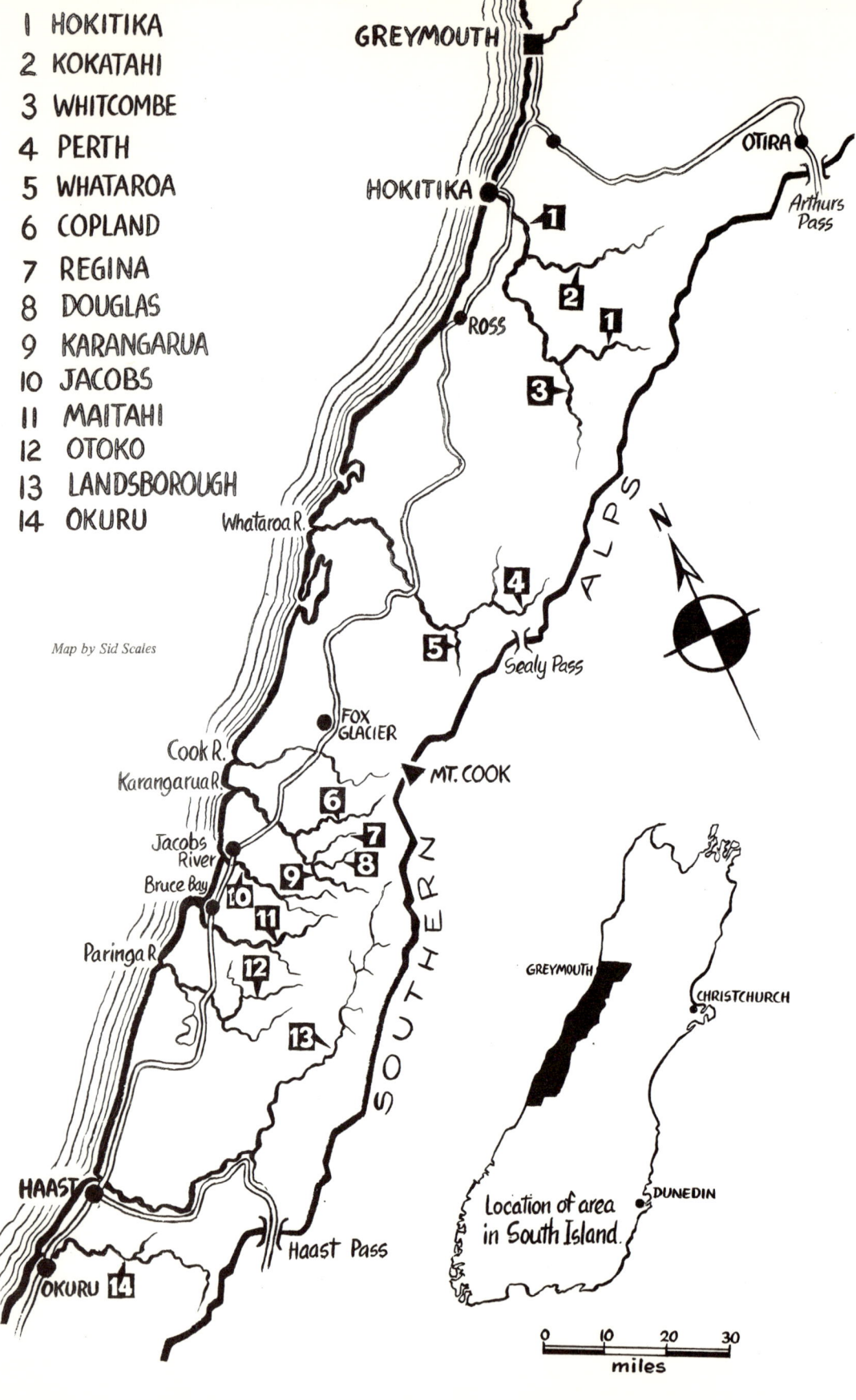

Map by Sid Scales

CONTENTS

		Page
	Preface	xi
	Introduction	xiii
1.	Bring 'Em Back Alive	1
2.	Up In The Air	10
3.	Anything Goes — Or Went	24
4.	The Old Firm	36
5.	Climbing High	48
6.	Luck Can Be A Lady	60
7.	Memories Are Made...	70
8.	Up The Creek	82
9.	They Went Thataway	94
10.	On Safari	106
11.	Retrospect	121
	Appendix: Handy Harker Hints	128

LIST OF ILLUSTRATIONS

	Page
Goodwin McNutt and Laurie Williams refuelling FH 1100	2
Live tahr readied for transport by air	2
Yearling chamois after capture	2
Helicopter shadow on snowfield	4
Tahr being unloaded at Fox Glacier	5
Tahr on the run, Gunn River area	5
Building wild-game enclosure	7
Dart-gun and ammunition	8
The Troyte, midwinter	9
Hughes 500 helicopter	11
Howard Smith with Piper Super Cub	11
Game viewed from shooter's seat in helicopter	12
Helicopter site in Otoko Valley	13
Meat-hunting, Wanganui River	13
Near the top, Hitchen Range	13
Chamois on Moonbeam Torrent Slip	14
Deer carcases on the aerial "hook"	17
Peter Hennessey, expert gutter	19
The result of a good day's shooting from the air	21
A base hut, Kea Flat	25
Interior decoration, Top Hut, Karangarua Valley	25
Reynolds Flat hut, Otoko river area	25
Airstrip-building, Upper Waitoto	28
Howard Smith collecting carcases	28
Living in a meatsafe, Toi Toi Flat	28
Barry Petrie at Cascade River	30
Rifle-sight in use as a telescope	30
Meat recovery by packhorse, Waitoto River area	32
Ernie Wilson collecting carcases with tractor and trailer	33
Bringing chamois back to Bonar Flat hut	34
Harker Pass, between Sawtooth Ridge and Mt Hitchen	37
Peter Harker, Alan Weir, Barry Petrie, Paul Bevernage	39
Ballance lake, named on the author's advice	39
Headwaters, Waitaha River	39
Stag killed by a fall, Waitaha Valley	41
Peter Billington, Katzenach Ridge	41
Reid Creek, Waitaha Valley	43
Chamois shooting off Seddon Col	43
Tommy Wilder collecting firewood, Hitchen Basin	43
Syme Lake, Waitaha Valley	46
Cliff Peart, Waitoto Valley	49
Packhorse dragging carcase	49
Deer shot near Drake River flats	49
Flannagans Peak	51
Crossing the Waitoto	51
Chamois, above Waitoto River	52
"Log cabin", Bonar Flat hut	52
Interior, Bonar Flat hut	52
Startled stag escaping	54
Indian-style canoe used on Mt Datamos trip	54
View of Waipara River	57
View from Knobs Point	58
Bannoch Brae Range	61
The late Tony Hawker	63
Attaching chains to helicopter	63
Hiller 12E helicopter with load	63
Ice ridge, Chainman's Creek	65
Miserable Ridge, Mikonui catchment area	65
Helicopter view at zero altitude	66
Ken Harker, the author's father, with Stuart Menzies and Peter Harker	68
Hard country, Whataroa River area	69
Flick Harrop crossing Adams River	71
Chamois shot at Architects Creek	73
Chamois, Headlong Spur	73
Overlooking Hot Springs Creek, Wanganui River area	73
Rope access, Lower Waitaha Valley	75
Stag alerted by sound of camera shutter	75
Lower Otoko Pass	77
Rough travelling, Hawkins Creek	77

LIST OF ILLUSTRATIONS — continued

	Page		Page
Chamois headskins, Valley of Darkness	79	Bull tahr trophy	113
Bruce Wright at Jacobs River	83	First animal (stag) shot with single-point sight	113
Edison headwaters from Barrier Cliff	83	Gene Bush and Bill Sands, American hunters	113
Deer at the head of the Edison	85	Open-air cookery, Regina Creek	115
Edison hut, Maitahi River	85	Author on Balfour Glacier	116
Brian Titheridge, "Popeye", Graham Allen, Barry Petrie, in Parnell Creek area	85	Gunn River area — too tough for visitors	116
Female chamois and kid, Morse River area	88	Chamois — an unorthodox shot	119
Bull tahr, Mueller Pass	88	Inaccessible country — till the helicopters arrived	122
Climbing after tahr, Scone Creek	88	Rutting deer, Edison country	123
Bettison Stream country	91	A close-range photo, Pollock Creek	123
George Lindsay and Jim Wilson, gutting tahr	92	Alan Weir and young friend	124
Ernie Wilson beats the heat	94	Young hind at close range	124
Deer shot in Karangarua Valley	96	Harry Hawker	125
Pat York floating carcase on inner-tube raft	97	Tom Paris, Little Waitaha Basin	125
Paul Bevernage on flying fox	97	Joe Crawford and Dave Barton	125
Female chamois, Tuke River	99	Trophy-class, Karangarua Valley	126
Two deer with one bullet, Hitchen Basin	100	Bruce Wright in rock shelter, Otoko Valley	129
Barry Petrie and stag waiting for helicopter	100	The Maitahi, before and during flood	130
Glacier pinnacles	100	Barry Petrie boulder-hopping, Upper Perth Valley	130
Prospectors Creek, Perth River	103	Cascade River Valley	132
Jim McEwan's stag, County Stream area	107	Rugged terrain, Otoko River	133
Chamois aplenty	108	Whiteout. Bruce Slater at Dry Creek	134
Deer photographed at closest range	109	Basil Detloft in deep snow, Mt Allen	134
The stag scared by Frank Elridge	109	Barry Petrie carrying deer	134
Two notable trophies, tahr and chamois	111	Shale country, Douglas River	136
		At the head of the Perth River	137

PREFACE

PETER HARKER has packed more than the average adventures of a whole lifetime into his thirty-three years and, while doing so, has become an expert on the hunting regions of South Westland, the toughest in New Zealand.

Physically, he was well suited to a high-country with pack and rifle: a lanky, well-knit frame, strong shoulders and legs, and above-average fitness. But the best hunters are those who are able to live in affinity with the bush, rivers and mountains, to understand and appreciate them in all their moods. Peter Harker learned to do this in a quite remarkable fashion.

He was born in Christchurch, became a prominent schoolboy athlete at Linwood High, and was introduced to hunting deer by his father, Ken Harker, in the mid-1950s. First, there was a BSA lever-action target rifle, and later a cut-down Long Tom .303, and the hunting was usually carried out in Canterbury's Lees Valley region. Peter shot his first deer as a lad of fifteen, and during his years as a dental technician he spent an increasing amount of his spare time in the bush. He took working holidays on the West Coast, whitebaiting and deerstalking, until the lure of the mountains, and of the game, became so insistent that he decided to move to Ross.

There was a breaking-in period while he accompanied seasoned hunters who knew the Coast areas intimately, but soon he developed enough confidence to move farther and farther afield on his own, covering eventually all the ranges of South Westland on foot and, later, by air. He established new tracks into some areas, reopened old trails and marked them, and then began writing a weekly article about his experiences for the *Christchurch Star Sports* under the general title of "Hunting With Harker".

As a hunting correspondent, and as a representative of the Lands and Survey Department providing mapping information on remote areas of the rugged Coast, he eventually covered the complete mountain range south from Hokitika, visiting the headwaters of every river and valley. Indeed, in some of the remoter areas his tracks and bivouacs are still in use, and some of his old campsites have been recorded and titled on official maps. There are streams, spurs, tarns, even a pass which carry the Harker name, or names suggested by him to the mapmakers.

Peter Harker's reputation spread beyond New Zealand hunting circles, largely as a result of his safari operations, and he was approached by overseas rifle and gun-sight manufacturing companies to test their equipment under the adverse weather conditions of the West Coast high country. He was, for instance, the first person in New Zealand to shoot a game animal — a large red stag — with the then new single-point sight.

When he began meat-hunting, game was plentiful in South Westland, and he and his companions made a reasonable living floating or back-packing carcases out of the bush to the road. Then fixed-wing aircraft and, later, helicopters were hired for game recovery, and he had a brief spell with a jetboat before it was wrecked on an expedition a short distance below the Ten Hour Gorge in the Arawata River. His frequent hunting mates during these years were Peter Billington, Barry Petrie and Paul Bevernage, and later still there was a character named Ernie Wilson: their names will crop up throughout this story. They had many, many adventures, and though their published expeditions occasionally drew criticisms from the purists against the unorthodox techniques sometimes used on the mountains or in river crossings, they suffered few serious accidents.

Peter Harker moved on to aerial shooting and game recovery with Winged Hunters Helicopter Ltd and other operators, worked as a safari guide for hunters from the United States, Australia, the United Kingdom, Japan, South Africa and New Zealand, and later began capturing animals live for game parks by jumping from hovering helicopters. As his reputation spread, so did the demand for his services and advice. He was always quick to point out that hunting on the eastern side of the Alps was a totally different experience from shooting on the West Coast: "The rain can turn small creeks into raging torrents within a very short time because of the sharp, steep fall from the mountains to the sea; and the bush is much more difficult, much denser," he told his clients. His advice still holds good: South Westland is no place for the novice.

Late in 1972 Peter Harker was offered a job with a sporting goods manufacturer in Michigan, USA, but opted to remain in New Zealand as manager-secretary for the Otago Acclimatisation Society in a different sphere of game management and administration. The decision to leave the bush was made easier because he had by now traversed his favourite areas so often that they were almost as wellknown to him as his own backyard. Some of the original challenge had disappeared.

When it was learned that he was leaving the Coast, Peter Harker was farewelled by the *New Zealand Outdoors* magazine in an article which said: "The West Coast of the South Island has lost one of the most controversial and publicised figures that has resided there since probably the goldrush days. In seven years Peter Harker climbed, mapped, hunted and tramped through every valley from the Hokitika River to the head of the Red Pike and Lake McKerrow . . . For the hundreds of people who were never refused information or skilfully drawn maps, and the many who were fortunate to join him in the field, we know they will miss his advice and companionship, and will be aware the West Coast of the South Island has lost somebody who was unique . . ."

That is a fair assessment of Harker the hunter. His new responsibilities limit his opportunities for hunting, but he still dons his bush gear during holiday breaks or tries his hand, and eye, from the helicopter step — always in South Westland, the region which holds a special place in his regard and which is the venue of all the experiences recorded in this book.

My task has been to try and capture the essence of the man's expertise in one of New Zealand's most rugged hunting regions and to select, from the hundreds of stories he can recall, a representative series which illustrate a unique career and which give some insight into the dramatic changes which have occurred in hunting, both recreational and professional, during the past decade. It is not a list of the "best places to shoot" because Peter Harker believes these change too rapidly under the pressure of modern game-recovery methods to be other than misleading now that he is not in constant touch with the conditions.

While an occasional word or phrase in this book may be mine, the ideas and experiences recorded here are entirely those of Peter Harker, hunter extraordinary.

Dunedin   Keith Eunson

INTRODUCTION

WHEN PETER HARKER stopped writing his regular hunting articles there was widespread disappointment among enthusiasts who sought their resumption. This was not possible, but he has relented to the extent of putting into more permanent form his reminiscences of his hunting days. The title of this book will be widely recognised, because it owes its origin to the *Christchurch Star* which carried it regularly every week for several years.

Peter and I have discussed whether, in these days of metrication, we should express ranges and distances in the old measures or the new. We decided on the old measures for two main reasons: hunters seem still to think in terms of feet and yards, and Peter's sense of recall was also in these terms. The more obvious heights — of mountains, for instance — have been converted to metrics, but in the main I have left the rest as Peter remembered them.

K.E.

CHAPTER ONE

BRING 'EM BACK ALIVE

THE HELICOPTER banked towards the herd of chamois grazing in the basin. I was perched on its step by the rear doorway, the early morning air knifing through my jacket like a razor blade as I waited for the herd to break and scatter. The constant womp... womp... of the rotor scared the animals. A fullgrown female with a halfgrown kid broke from their companions and scampered towards the cover of a jumble of rocks.

As Goodwin McNutt straightened the machine to follow this pair, I braced myself on the step. The female and her kid made the rock shelter and crouched in hiding. The ground below me blurred as we flew in low. As we came level with the rock-pile McNutt banked the machine, and when I judged we were due to pass over the pair of chamois I jumped... my feet hit the top of a boulder which gave me the leverage to bounce forward to grab the female at the base of her needle-sharp horns, and the kid by a leg.

The scuffle was brief and exciting. There was really no time for thinking: action sprang from instinct and experience. So while I held on to the two chamois, McNutt landed the helicopter nearby and came over with the tranquilliser to quieten them so we could carry them safely out to our base at Fox Glacier.

This was hunting with a *difference*. It was a form of game capture designed for a specific purpose in very difficult terrain, and one which I certainly do not recommend for any but the very fit — and perhaps the very foolish!

Goodwin McNutt had previously carried out live-game capture from helicopters in the North Island, but it was while I was working with his Winged Hunters organisation that we introduced this particular method into the South Island for chamois and tahr and, occasionally, for deer when game parks wanted them. On the east coast or other flatlands the use of tranquiliser darts was a safe and easy means of capture. The animals could be followed for miles until the drug took effect and they rolled over; but in the South Westland high country, habitat of the chamois and tahr, tranquilised animals could all too easily be lost by falling over bluffs or rolling into dense scrub, and we considered it better for the animals, and generally more effective from our own viewpoint, to take them in an aerial rugby tackle.

The technique was demanded by the conditions in which we operated, and we developed and perfected it on a trial-and-error basis until it was virtually fool-

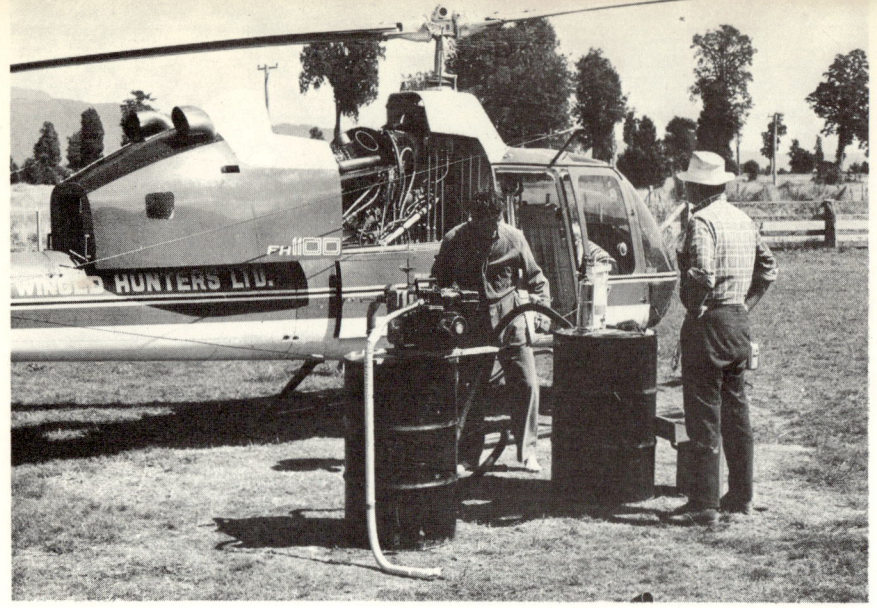

Well-known Westland personality Goodwin McNutt, assisted by Laurie Williams, refuels the FH 1100.

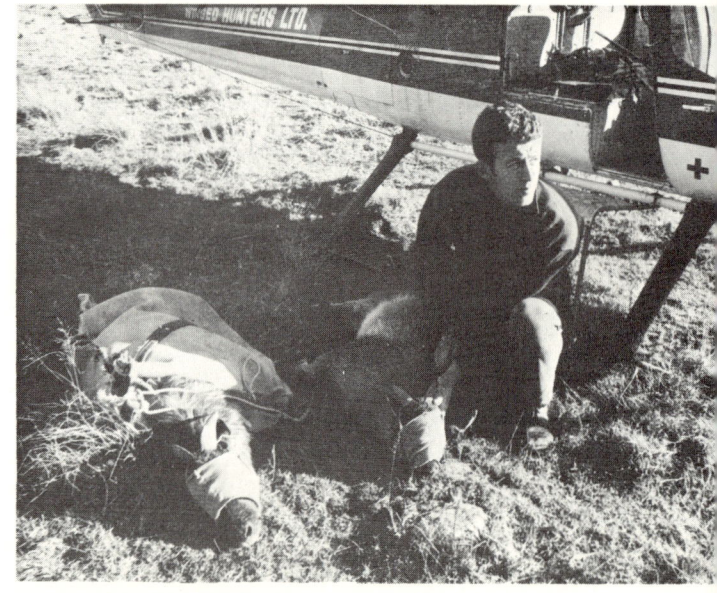

Young tahr, blindfolded and wrapped in their special carrying-bags by Les Mahn, ready for the flight to Fox Glacier.

A yearling chamois captured by the author in the head of the Lords River.

proof. On one occasion I recall we captured ten animals in an hour — by far our best catch, yet an illustration nonetheless of how smooth the operation had become. Generally, when we had orders to fill for live game we could be reasonably assured of taking ten or so a day, and during the year or more I was engaged in this form of capture we could have taken a total of 100-150 from the high country.

There was a very keen demand for live game at the time, particularly from game parks, and we had ideas as well for exporting animals — until we ran up against Department of Agriculture regulations. However, domestic demand and the prices being paid were such that the risks involved were worthwhile. Chamois brought from $150 to $250 each, depending on size and quality, while tahr could be sold for $450 a pair. And there was an added value when live-game capture could be combined with safari operation: if we could move in and capture live game while flying overseas visitors to or from hunting areas, they certainly had something unusual to talk about when they met their hunting mates back home in the United States, Japan or Australia. It was good for business.

However, the high rate of capture and the good prices paid for live game didn't mean that the operation was all profit. Far from it at times. Overheads in operating an FH 1100 jet helicopter were considerable, but it was the numerous pitfalls about which we knew little or nothing until we had fallen into them that caused most of our problems. Although financial returns were generally better than for commercial meat-shooting, animal losses tended often to be high when we started, especially those caused by bringing high-country wild animals to the flatlands where they became disorientated and, with plenty of grazing available, tended to gorge themselves and scour badly.

There was as well the shock of capture. This affected animals of different age groups in an astonishingly different way. For instance, a fully grown bull tahr might appear completely to adjust to his new environment and go on thriving for weeks or even months, only to fold without warning... just roll over and die without any apparent reason. Others put into a wire enclosure might tear full tilt at it and break their necks, or injure themselves so severely they had to be put down. And they never seemed to learn; they had had no experience of fences in the high country.

We also discovered that animals put into open enclosures sometimes turned vicious and attacked their fellows; and there were always the problems of sickness. Indeed, we soon discovered that the knowledge we had picked up about game animals as stalkers or professional hunters was totally inadequate for live-game capture, and in this new field we had to learn which animals adjusted best — and how to assist them orientate to their new circumstances so that the mortality rate was brought under control.

Perhaps our most important breakthrough occurred when we began isolating newly-captured animals in a darkened shed for several days. The system worked both for single animals and for groups, and after a short period of this form of isolation we could almost hand-feed them like domestic animals. Indeed, those who

These chamois being transported by closed van do not seem unduly disturbed, but game animals do not always adjust so quickly to a new environment.

visit the game park at Fox Glacier run by Goodwin McNutt can see animals captured in the wild following him around the fenced enclosures like pet lambs — tahr bulls as well as chamois and deer.

The capture operation developed in Winged Hunters was to look for a good basin where there was some rocky terrain, so that it was possible either to jump down on to the animals or to wait behind the rock-piles until they were driven into their shelter. The FH 1100 jet has front and rear seats like a motorcar, and our jumps were made from the rear step, behind the pilot.

My own special equipment for handling captured animals once I had them in hand included a supply of old football socks with the toes cut from them. These had an elastic strip looped at one end so they could be pulled over the eyes of the animal and anchored in place behind the horns. I stuffed the socks down my shirt, while on my belt I had a supply of dog collars which I used to strap together the animals' feet to stop them from kicking.

If we were able to cut a chamois female and a youngster from a group of animals, the mother would stay with her kid and it was possible on occasions to capture two animals at the one time. The chamois kid, about the size of a Labrador retriever, could be held with the larger animal until help arrived when the helicopter landed.

This is, quite obviously, not a form of hunting to be undertaken without rigid training to achieve top fitness, and without proper planning. There are quite enough pitfalls for the experienced, let alone the tyros, and I lost a lot of skin off my arms, legs and back, and gained some massive abrasions and bumps while wrestling with animals, or from jumping when the chopper was too high, or in misjudging the leap, or in being bowled over by determined animals before I had properly set

Shadow on the snow. . . .

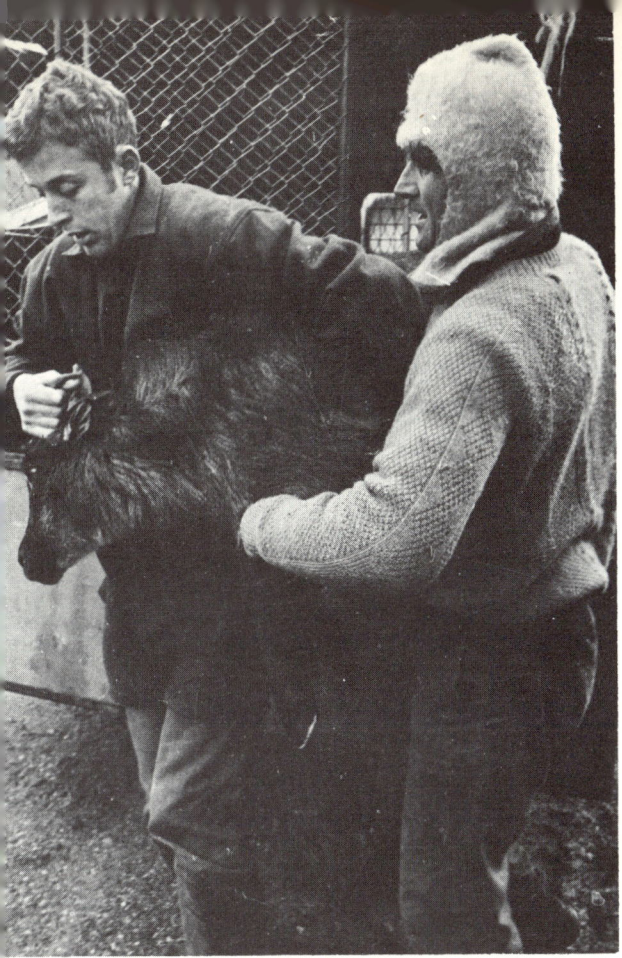
A female tahr captured at the head of Jacobs River being unloaded back at Fox Glacier by Les Mahn and Goodwin McNutt.

Tahr on the run from the helicopter in the Gunn River region.

myself for the capture. Chamois horns are needle-sharp, and there could often be real difficulties when they decided to charge with the head held well down. This required going in low like a rugby player to knock the legs from under the animal while trying to gain a grip behind the horns. If they came with the head up, it was much easier to go for them under the neck.

I recall an occasion in 1971 when we were operating from the Whataroa area. McNutt swept the machine down the Gunn watershed and we were amazed at the density of the chamois. There were mobs of them everywhere, and some of the bucks sported fine heads . . . a tempting sight to the hunter. But our programme on that occasion called for tahr, so we flew back over the Whataroa-Perth river junction and up into the Hughes Basin, where again there were plenty of chamois, but no tahr. This was a far cry from the previous year.

We jetted on past the entrance to the Scone Creek and up into Prospector's Basin where tahr were finally sighted. Although there was a liberal coating of snow on the ground — it was early August — and the mountain slopes glistened with ice, the groups of tahr were high and moving higher. We flew on into the Bettison, and at the top there seemed to be tahr everywhere. One large mob had about eight bulls for which a trophy hunter would have risked his right arm, given a chance at any one of them.

McNutt eased the chopper towards the basin floor, sorting out a large female to cut from the bunch. Once separated, she galloped down the edge of the fast-flowing river towards a narrow pass at the far end of the valley, showing no signs of slowing. McNutt flew on to the gap ahead of the tahr and left me there before zooming off to prevent her from breaking back to escape our capture plan. Meanwhile, I positioned myself behind a boulder, poised to spring as soon as she came bounding through the gap. And when she did appear, I was dismayed to see she had plenty of wind left — and I had a presentiment of what was going to happen.

I launched myself in a head-on flying tackle, but it was like leaping at a speeding locomotive. She didn't even break stride as she bowled me over backwards, leaving me lamenting amongst the rocks. However, pride was assuaged to an extent later when we managed to take her further down the basin and wrapped her up in one of the special canvas carrying-bags before flying back to tackle a bull.

This big bull had obviously made up his mind that the noisy machine was not going to take him, and we had problems buzzing him off the bluffs and setting him galloping towards open ground. The secret was to encourage the game to have a reasonable run to tire them sufficiently for the hunter to have the advantage, and from our height in the chopper we could pinpoint the groups of rocks likely to be used by the animals for their final stand. McNutt dropped me off at one of these rock-piles and flew off to round up this bull tahr. He proved troublesome. After taking a breather he jumped into the river and, with only his head and free-flowing mane visible above the water, he stood there snorting and whistling defiance. He was a fine animal, but eventually that icy current must have proved too much for him because he climbed out of the water and made for the rocks where I was hiding.

As he passed my perch I flung myself down on his hindquarters and we hit the ground together. With only his front legs free, escape was impossible so he was soon injected and bagged for the flight back to Whataroa.

Goodwin McNutt was one of the pioneers of game recovery, using fixed-wing aircraft in the North Island before moving on to helicopters, and he had tried several methods of live-game capture. In the North Island he had used nets which he dropped on to the animals, and he has used this method with some success in the South Island as well. As I stated earlier, the opportunities for using tranquilliser guns are limited in the South Westland region because of the rugged nature of the country, but there are some areas where they can be used and where we brought them into use.

One of the first occasions is printed indelibly on my mind because of the immense beauty of the day we went flying — and because I was trying out new equipment. The sun had not yet risen over the snowladen peaks of Cook and Tasman. They stood out in vivid relief against a red dawn sky as we gained height for the day's operation. It was a sight to remember — and one to sadden as well, in

McNutt and Barry Petrie build a wild-game enclosure to avoid damage to animals from their running into wire fences.

that I lacked the artistic skills to capture those few minutes of absolutely superb beauty.

But the sadness was in retrospect. At the time there were other interests and other demands: a Paxarm gas-powered dart gun which had once belonged to an African National Park team and had played its part in saving hundreds of animals threatened by the rising waters of a newly-built dam. So I became fully engaged with the statistics of dart velocity related to trajectory which I had tested on the ground over ranges from 50 feet to 500 feet using leather targets to gauge penetration.

The rising sun saturated the peaks as we moved into our hunting territory, and two chamois catapulted out from the tall snow tussock, disturbed by the clatter of our rotors. As the distance narrowed, I eased the rifle butt firmly into my shoulder and flicked the telescopic lens cap off. Through this special 6-power 'scope I measured off the distance on the trajectory scale alongside the cross-hair. At 30 feet a squeeze on the trigger produced a muffled "plop" as the dart left the rifle. I saw it strike home, and that was chamois No. 1 . . . and there were to be seven others that day. But it was not always so simple — or so successful.

Life was never boring, however. On one occasion while live-game catching along the Fritz Ridge we spotted a pair of chamois diving into a cave as we flew over a moraine field. McNutt took the machine close in and dropped me off near the entrance to the cave, which he lit with the helicopter's powerful nose light. When I looked inside, the chamois stood snorting and wheezing, defying me to approach closer. The larger of the pair was thrusting forward, moving those sharp horns

The Paxarm gas-powered dart-gun, used originally to rescue game from the Kariba Dam (Africa) area. On his first use of it in South Westland the author captured eight animals.

backwards and forwards in readiness for battle. Outside I could hear the hovering helicopter.

I shuffled toward the chamois with arms outstretched, my eyes glued on those horns. And then, as though by private signal, both animals charged together, and I had no time to worry about being gored. As the larger one got within grasping distance I flung myself on to its neck, bringing it down with the momentum of the charge. One horn ripped into the side of my wrist and cut along it before catching in the base of a finger. But the final victory was mine. Within minutes the chamois was blindfolded, tranquillised and ready for transport out, while I dragged heavily on a cigarette and licked my wounds.

On another occasion while shooting in the Lords River area at the head of the Lambert, we located a mob of chamois and were getting in behind them when a pair dived down a hole in the rocks. They had corralled themselves, as it were, and the opportunity for live capture was too promising to pass up. As McNutt brought the machine in close I leaped out and rushed over to the pile of boulders. Peering down the hole I could see two sets of beady eyes glaring up at me. In reaching into the darkness I was several inches short of getting a grip on either animal. Idiotic though it was on later reflection, I lowered myself down the hole on to the chamois and this brought a spice of chaos to the situation. I could feel the animals fighting furiously beneath me. The sharp point of a horn scraped the inside of my leg and dug in. I twisted and kicked outwards, freeing my leg, and then dropped back, eventually subduing both animals.

In July 1971 we were shooting tahr at the head of the Douglas River and had flown up the edge of an ice-covered lake when we spotted a mob on the lip of a snowfield sweeping towards the edge of a large plateau. McNutt brought the machine in level and swung round to give me a clear field of fire, and I was just about to bag a big bull tahr when he motioned me to hold. Some of the animals had run into the open and were floundering in the soft snow. Leading the charge was a really fine female tahr

Midwinter in the Troyte, but the hunt goes on from the air.

of exactly the type needed for the game park harem at Fox Glacier. That decided it. McNutt dropped me off where I could see the tahr ploughing around in a deepish drift. I mushed forward in the knee-deep snow and was about to grab the female tahr when she bounded forward a few paces. Not to be outdone I thrashed my way forward again and made a mighty leap. The result was rather like running slap into a brick wall.

In spite of it all I hung grimly on, tangled up in hair, legs, snow and pounding hooves, and managed eventually to get a blindfold on to her. On that particular trip Vic Eckhoff (now of Taumarunui, I believe) was sitting in the front passenger seat beside Goodwin McNutt, filming the whole scene with a movie camera, so he should have a laugh-a-minute film show whenever he shows it.

Meanwhile, for those who may feel the odds of machine and man against animals in live-game capture are unfair, I have permanent evidence on arms and legs to prove that the hunter doesn't always win.

These game animals are regarded officially as pests and there is a virtual price on their heads. However, in my observation those taken to game parks adjust fairly quickly to the restrictions on their freedom, and they have almost certainly avoided death at the hands of the commercial meat-hunters.

Further, animals captured live are selected for their quality, so only good specimens are retained. And who knows . . . these animals in game parks and on deer farms might be the only ones seen by the general public in future, because the destruction rate of game in South Westland alone is still around 50,000 animals a year.

CHAPTER TWO

UP IN THE AIR

HELICOPTERS HAVE given a new dimension to game control in New Zealand, despite what the recreational hunter might claim in their disfavour. Indeed, when the role of the helicopter is evaluated in the wider field of operation it can be shown to have made a significant contribution, but most notably as a means of control leading to some measurable improvement in ground cover in specific regions which simply could never have been achieved by traditional culling methods of sending in teams of hunters on foot. What has been achieved by helicopters operated by commercial meat-recovery concerns would have required an army of foot shooters and an organisation quite beyond the manpower or financial resources of the New Zealand Forest Service.

It is New Zealand's good fortune, in fact, that there is a reasonable price for game meats, for without an economic game-recovery industry the commercial helicopters would at once disappear and the full charge for control measures would fall back on the taxpayer. And in this regard I tend to agree with a view expressed by Mr J.T. Holloway, Director of the Forestry Protection Branch, Rangiora, that any slackening of effort for a few years "could well set us back twenty years or more".

The control and management of game make little impact on the public at large, but they have become a bone of contention between officialdom and the recreational shooter as represented by the New Zealand Deerstalkers' Association. The issue is control versus management, and the helicopter operator tends to be caught somewhere in the middle, winning more adverse than favourable publicity. Yet besides providing an efficient culling operation at an absolute minimal cost to the taxpayer, the helicopter has also been the means of establishing a multimillion-dollar industry earning foreign exchange from game-meat exports — an advantage which has been largely obscured from public view by the overblown storm about the so-called "helicopter war", and the sometimes ill informed criticism from recreational hunters, particularly those abroad whose opinions too often are based on films of deer carcases hanging from the chains beneath helicopters on their way to the processing factories, or of shooters "enjoying" the benefit of an aerial platform to bowl over game right, left and centre.

These points should be clarified at once. First, deer, chamois and tahr have been declared noxious animals in New Zealand because they multiplied at such an alarming rate as to threaten soil cover and forests. The law decrees that these

A Hughes 500 helicopter, one of several types utilised as aerial shooting platforms in South Westland. Hiller helicopters are also popular.

One of the best known pilots on the West Coast, Howard Smith, graduated from fixed-wing aircraft to helicopters. He is shown here with his Piper Super Cub, loaded with game, on a Landsborough strip.

animals, as pests, must be shot out to an extent yet to be decided; after which management policies may take over from present control methods. Secondly, helicopters have enabled shooting to be carried out in areas seldom penetrated by cullers or recreational hunters on foot, and for the shot animals to be recovered and sold for general benefit. Thirdly, the least understood fact about helicopter shooting is that it is hard, dangerous work carried out usually in isolated areas of the South Island, and in conditions which no 40-hour-a-week union man would deign to accept.

It is certainly not a case of a professional marksman sitting in the comfort of a padded seat bowling game with a stream of lead. There are plenty of natural hazards in any sort of flying, but these are multiplied up when operating in the rough high country of South Westland and they exert a constant strain on pilot and shooter, requiring from them long periods of concentration, often at high altitudes, plus the ever-present risk of mechanical malfunction. There is as well the likelihood of injury, or worse, in manhandling animals ready for pickup from dangerous ice-covered areas in the tops, so my advice to anyone who believes helicopter meat recovery work is just a careless, adventurous life that pays big money for a minimum of work, is to try it for a week and learn the real facts the hard way.

It might emphasise my point to show that in 1973-74 helicopters operating in New Zealand had an accident rate of 18.1 crashes for each 10,000 hours flown (the

Two seconds to live... a view of game (*in circle*) from the shooter's seat.

international yardstick) compared with 1.6 crashes for fixed-wing aircraft. Many of these accidents occurred in mountainous country where, because of their versatility, helicopters are more likely to be used. Thus the tendency is for them to be exposed to more accident-prone situations. Of the twenty-two helicopter accidents which occurred, two thirds of them involved meat-recovery operations.

As far as the "helicopter war" was concerned, there is no doubt that, particularly in the Fiordland region where small operators felt they were being squeezed out unfairly in favour of the big company operation, there was widespread poaching, illegal shooting and recovery, and instances of malpractice. But in South Westland where I flew with Alpine Helicopters, Whirlwide Helicopters and Winged Hunters, there was a highly competitive spirit which did sometimes lead to hard words in a hotel bar, but to no instances of any "dirty work at the cross-roads", in my experience anyway.

This was not true, however, of fixed-wing plane operations. I know of cases where isolated landing strips had holes dug across them; and of at least one instance where fencing wire was strung between trees at a height which would catch the undercarriage of an aircraft and flip it. If the culprits had been found, the other operators and crews in the district would have dealt with them in their own inimitable way!

Helicopter hunting is really only a decade old in New Zealand. Commercial venison recovery began here in the late 1950s, and carcases were brought out then by the best means available: by utilising horses, tractors, or boats, floating them down rivers on old truck tubes, or carrying them on the back like a sack of potatoes. Fixed-wing planes made the job easier and quicker (although a lot of hard labour went into carving out rough strips for landing in the wild country) and helicopters later made the operation even more flexible. Still, it wasn't until around 1964 that helicopters began regularly to be used as aerial platforms for shooting and thus promoted venison and other game meat-recovery into a thriving export industry. Indeed, it was 1964-65 that the game kill, on official figures, topped 50,000 animals for export for the first time.

The value of the helicopter is its manoeuvrability and its ability to set down anywhere such as at this spot in the Otoko Valley to secure game.

Meat-hunting in the Wanganui River in 1969 gave the author one of his best hourly kills: sixteen animals within an hour.

Near the top of the Hitchen Range, very difficult country for shooters.

A chamois on Moonbeam Torrent Slip, Waitaha River.

In recent years the export of game has been running at about 100,000 carcases a year, though the good years may temporarily be over because of the much tighter hygiene regulation requirements introduced by the West German Government — and because the economics of aerial shooting have tilted against the operator in the past year or so. There is a shortage of accessible game to keep the expensive machines in the air.

When George Lindsay, a Maniototo farmer, accompanied me back to the Coast during May 1975, Goodwin McNutt flew us from Fox Glacier to the head of the Cook and we saw few animals from the air. Yet on virtually the same flight pattern a year earlier we had had no problems sighting chamois, particularly, counting twenty-two on one ninety-minute flight. At that time aerial teams were having to work hard for their returns, but they were still making out.

It is different now. We actually saw helicopters returning after a five-hour stint with only three animals slung beneath the machine, and one operator told us how he spent a day and a-half in the Whataroa-Perth area for twenty chamois and tahr.

A friend who had been working southern Westland by helicopter for a couple of years had withdrawn his machine when George and I got there in May because he could not maintain economic returns. Whereas he needed 200lbs of meat per flying hour, he had been taking between 130 and 160lbs maximum. He keeps in touch with the situation, and a fellow operator told him he had recently been in the air for seven hours for a return of eight deer.

Yet make no mistake about it: there are still deer about. In my view the wily old customers have become helicopter-wise. George and I walked up the Maitahi to the Plateau hut on our first night and I shot one of the three deer we saw within a ten-minute stroll of the hut. The next day we spent about eight hours around the region and spotted twenty or so deer in the bush. George was able to move in with his movie camera to a reasonably close distance to photograph a stag and five hinds. But the deer are alert to the noise of helicopters, and move into the bush where they remain immobile until the noise diminishes.

During a visit to the tops during the 1974-75 holiday season I noticed the grass had come back and was waist-high, yet there was virtually no deer sign around the tarns. On the big riverflats there was plenty of sign near the bush, indicating just how well educated game has become to the helicopter. I spoke about it to a former hunting companion, Ernie Wilson, who had been spotlighting up the Arawata; he reported counting a dozen deer on the flats during the night trip, but during the day these flats are deserted.

I believe there are still plenty of deer for the skilled bushstalker who wants to visit southern Westland, though trophy animals are few and far between. Those of trophy standard seem to have moved to the coastal swamps for some reason, and Alan Weir (ace shooter for Alpine Helicopters Ltd) said he had picked up a 12-pointer there during mid-March. But up around the heads of the Douglas, Regina, Copland, Karangarua, Troyte and other areas well known for their game trophy potential a few years earlier, there is virtually nothing of note being taken now.

Goodwin McNutt told me he had flown a party of North Island hunters into the head of the Regina for a two-week safari, but they had walked out after a week, having shot one chamois and seen only a couple of others. Another footshooter I know actually spent five days around the head of the Karangarua and got nothing. He never even fired a shot! . . .

Quite obviously the tops have been shot out by the helicopters. Yet erosion continues in many of the valleys, as it will do from natural (as well as noxious) causes where there is so high a rainfall. The biggest threat to afforestation today in my view is the opossum, which is settled into the area from sea level right up to the alpine bush. Brian Leckie, wellknown as a 'possum hunter', told me he is getting his best results from areas above the 3,000 ft level.

There are still markets for game caught and handled to an acceptable hygiene formula, but the deer, chamois and tahr are proving increasingly elusive. The years of heaviest shooting — those when prices were highest — obviously knocked the game population back to a considerable degree, and the time may well be right to consider the future. If the commercial operator is forced out because meat hunting is no longer profitable, then some other means of control will need to be found.

I had used helicopters for getting game out of the tops before I actually started shooting from them. When shooting on foot up the Karangarua, Kiwi Flat in the Waitaha River, Bald Hill above the Mikonui, the Edison River and Jacobs River I had called in choppers to lift out meat, as well as for bringing in gear for summer camps and the like.

But my first actual experience of shooting from the air came early in 1968. Late the previous year I had been foot shooting for chamois in the head of Hot Springs

Creek, a tributary of the Wanganui, with Tom Paris as a companion. We had seen a number of goodlooking deer and I filed the region away in my mind for future reference. So when Clive Maitland arrived down from Wellington the following February seeking a good stag or two, we decided to try the large hanging basin near the head of Hot Springs Creek. We had entered by way of Speculation Ridge and taken a long slog around the tops where there was a ton of game . . . deer, hinds, spikers and stags up to 8 points, but none of the really big stuff we'd been expecting.

Until this time the only helicopter activity I had observed on the Coast was the occasional machine passing up or down the beaches between Hokitika and Haast, operated by Graham Stewart's organisation, so it came as a surprise to see a Bell helicopter fly into our basin and begin shooting the edge before landing near our camp, which was sited in the middle of the open area. The pilot, an American, asked if I was familiar with the Wanganui and I told him I knew the catchments of the area, from the head of the Evans to the head of the Adams, fairly well. This led to an invitation to spend a few hours in the air pointing out the likely game areas.

I readily agreed. Ride in a helicopter . . . big thrill!

At this time there were comparatively few deer in the heads of these rivers. The Adams was reasonably well known for good stags, though these were few and far between. They just didn't appear to favour settling right up in the heads of the valleys. However, leaving Hot Springs Creek we flew across to a place called Cairnback and got on to several mobs of deer, with about a dozen animals in each. The first lot were shot by the young Maori shooter on the machine, and while he flew out with these I remained to gut the remainder ready for the next pickup. But the chopper returned without the shooter and I was invited to spend the rest of the afternoon behind the gun.

We flew into the head of the Amethyst Ravine — and it was in the basin there that I shot my first deer from a helicopter. It was February, 1968. But I soon discovered that aerial shooting was much more awkward than I'd expected it to be. At the time I was using a .303 and the 'scope was a 4-power Lyman with a very fine cross-hair, not well suited to shooting from helicopters, but after using up a lot of ammunition I got a load of seven or eight deer before continuing with my ground companion, Clive Maitland, back at Hot Springs Creek.

It was not until the following August that I got another chance at airborne shooting. I had spent two successful days hunting near the trig station on Mt Wilberg around the tops to a point overlooking the Porerua River, and had shot ten animals, gutted them and walked out to ring Graham Stewarts to arrange a helicopter pickup. I met the machine at Hendes Ferry the next morning and we were able to recover all but two of my deer. The pilot then asked me to fill in an hour or so shooting from the helicopter, so after removing the 9-power 'scope I'd been using we flew over the range of flat open country known locally as Terriquin. Although hampered by low cloud we managed to get three stags, one of them a 14-pointer of considerable size. At this time, in 1968, chamois were extremely plentiful, and

This meat-recovery illustration has upset some overseas and local sportsmen. The deer on the hook are from the Cook Range, south of Fox Glacier.

though there were no really large herds visible, groups were consistent throughout the region. However, major interest at that time was in deer and not the chamois.

The following June when John Hardy, Robbie Scott and Joe Whitman, an Australian, were camped with me at Mt Barry a period of bad weather forced us down Headlong Spur into Bertram Creek where we re-established camp on a spur more or less overlooking the head of Whirling Water. Here we noticed a helicopter shooting up the tussock tops of Uruguay Knob and the eastern slopes of Mt Hitchen. It later flew down to our camp and we had a chat with the pilot while his gutter finished with the animals they had shot. He was very interested when we told him of a mob of deer living up at the head of Scamper Torrent, and within minutes he had invited me to join him to go for a look, armed with Joe Whitman's 7mm carbine and about twenty bullets. We shot five deer before I ran out of ammunition, but I remembered this flight particularly because the company later sent me a cheque for £10 (about $20) . . . something which other pilots had promised but forgotten about after the excitement of the hunt.

And then again, about November, I was invited to spend several hours shooting from a helicopter in the high country at the head of the Mikonui and the head of the Tuke, probably one of the first times this region had been shot from a helicopter. It was certainly on this assumption we based our expectation that returns would be high. The permanent shooter on the machine at this time was Bob (Noddy) Nicholson and it was he who invited me to go along. The day was perfect, clear and calm, but we saw few animals although I knew from expeditions on the ground that they were numerous on the tops. Yet during three hours we spent in the air I saw only twenty or so deer, and managed to shoot about a dozen of them.

During those earlier years helicopter activity was confined almost wholly to high, open tussock country; slips and open patches in the bush, or creekbeds, were simply not bothered with because of the difficulties involved. Deer were taken off the easy country where they could be collected after shooting with a minimum of trouble. Today, however, a totally different situation exists because helicopter shooting pressure and the number of machines operating, coupled with the high cost of operating require helicopter crews to take deer from wherever they can find them. And since prices for venison have plunged way below the dollar-a-pound level of the boom year, "wherever they can find them" means just that.

In March, 1970, while hunting the Haast Range and various valleys in the region, the Thomas, Clarke and Macfarlane, deer were plentiful and our tallies per hour were usually five or six. Some of the sets of antlers left on the tops would have broken a trophy hunter's heart to leave; I remember particularly a very large and even 16-pointer shot in the Clarke River near Marks Flat which would have gone 40 x 40 without much difficulty, while at our gut pile there were numerous antlers in the range of 12s and 10s which would have been better than 38 x 38. Yet when I walked along those tops again in 1971 I could find no antlers and, indeed, no signs that numerous deer had been gutted there, especially above Kea Bluffs and the

One of the characters of the meat-hunting days was Peter Hennessey, known affectionately as Dracula because of his ability to gut a deer in twelve seconds. He was lightning with a gutting knife.

head of Clarke River, overlooking the mid-section of the Landsborough, where I particularly remembered leaving some decent-sized heads.

And so in June of 1971 I met Goodwin McNutt, for whom I was to shoot on numberous occasions for Winged Hunters Ltd . . . red deer, chamois and tahr. We first shot the frontal high country between the Cook River and the Karangarua and took a lot of animals there before moving into the Karangarua itself and gaining success in the Troyte, at the head of the main river itself and in the Copland. At that time I was using a Savage .308 lever action with rotating magazine which proved a curse as far as loading was concerned. It was worst in the early morning when sitting on the exposed step of the helicopter in near-freezing conditions trying to thumb rounds into the rotary mag. with numb fingers. Yet we always seemed to manage somehow.

I remember once when flying into the Troyte accompanied by Brian Titheridge, we saw a reasonably scattered mob of deer and, because of the area in which they were holed up, it was decided that I should be dropped off on a high vantage point and the machine used to round them up. This assumed that I would be able to snipe away with greater certainty of success. Anyway, I sighted on the group, picked the nearest animal, lined it up in the 'scope and squeezed the trigger. Two deer collapsed, the first time I had taken two with one bullet.

Unknown to us at that time, a party of stalkers had camped in a bush area at the Troyte basin and were just making preparations for a day's shooting when we arrived and cleaned the area out. We learned this later from a critical newspaper article in which helicopter operations were condemned, and the finger was pointed at our blue-and-white machine in particular. It might be some compensation to those hunters to learn even now that of the deer we shot in the Troyte during that period none was of trophy standard. In fact, as far as my own experiences in the Karangarua were concerned, I can recall only two reasonably-sized heads we did take from a considerable amount of flying.

When operating with Winged Hunters one of our favourite jaunts was to fly directly up the Cook River and pass over the range into a section of Architect's Creek, where we could often take deer off the flats before moving on to the Regina. Here we were usually sure of getting half a dozen more. It was while shooting from a helicopter in the Regina that I bagged my first hummel deer — a male which does not grow antlers — but it was not until the gutting stage I realised it was not a hind.

Looking back now on those days in the air there are experiences I would rather not have had when death, or at least serious injury, seemed to be staring me in the face, yet they were part and parcel of the life of a professional hunter, and talks I have had with others before and since suggest that they were, and are, the sort of thing which the helicopter crews are facing all the time. Everyone who goes hunting in the high country of South Westland needs skill and experience — but those who fly in day after day need the balance of fortune tilted their way as well.

I remember an incident early on when we were in the head of the Perth River shooting from a Hiller 12E machine which had seen better days. We had shot some six fullgrown bull tahr in a very tight creek, and because of the snow conditions it was impossible to drag them into a reasonably open area for collection by the machine. However, I fixed about 60 feet of wire chain on to the chopper's hook and made my way on foot down the steep slope into the creek where the animals were pulled into a pile. A nylon strop went through the rear hocks and then I signalled to the pilot that I was ready to collect.

He moved in, but the trailing rope remained tantalisingly just beyond the reach of my arm as I endeavoured to fix the clip to it so the animals could be pulled out. Just as I prepared to lunge again to fix the clip I heard a tremendous WHOOMP . . . WHOOMP . . . WHOOMP and flicked a glance up to see the rotor blades chopping into the snow on one side of the steep bench of the creek. I had nowhere to run to and fully expected to see the Hiller drop on to me, but fortunately the snow was powdered and had no rocks sticking through it, and we lived to fly another day.

In helicopter operations so much depends on the skill and concentration of the pilot; he often puts in long hours when flying conditions are right, because there can be weeks on the Coast when flying conditions are all wrong and no shooting is possible. There was an occasion in Prospectors Creek when trying to pick up tahr I had shot which still gives me the willies when I think of it. The helicopter hovered while I gutted the animals ready for the collection, and the pilot was watching me through the rear vision mirror on the skid. I just happened to look back while turning an animal, and saw the tail rotor only inches from an outcrop of rock. I yelled and pointed to the pilot who, fortunately, picked the situation immediately and moved the machine out without panic, but I was sweating nonetheless — and I'm not sure it was all due to the work of gutting those tahr.

A somewhat similar though much more frightening occasion occured once when a former schoolteacher of the pilot I was working with turned up with his camera, eager for a flight on the newfangled flying machine. We settled him inside and went

The result of a good day's shooting from the air in the Arawata River area in 1971.

after chamois, being fortunate enough to come on to a mob quite early in the piece, and to bowl a few of them over. The pilot picked a flat landing spot close to a gully. He left the machine ticking over quietly while I collected and gutted the catch, and he slipped down the gully to retrieve a chamois which had tumbled over. Unknown to either of us, the schoolteacher got out of the machine, and walked behind it to watch me gutting animals. When I heard a strangled sort of cry from the pilot, I looked up. As he had dragged the chamois over the top of the gully, he saw the schoolteacher slowly back-stepping towards the tail rotor as he sought to frame me in his camera shot. Another step or two into that whirling rotor and the schoolteacher would have been sliced up like meat going into a circular saw. The pilot was absolutely furious. With hardly a word the schoolteacher disappeared into the machine, into the distance. When the helicopter returned it had no passenger.

But there were traps for the experienced as well as the tyros, something I discovered while shooting from the air up the Balfour River. We had a pile of animals on the gut heap ready to lift out to the road. As the helicopter lifted off, I didn't move quickly enough. The game, because of the way in which they were tied, swung upside down during the early part of the machine's lift and the horns of a chamois dug into the side of my boot. This swept me upside down like the chamois, but fortunately I escaped with a ripped sock. I have heard of shooters being caught in this manner and lifted into the air, unknown to the pilot, and dropped from dangerous heights.

As soon as I begin thinking back to those days in the air, the memories keep crowding in, some funny, some sad, and some just downright crazy. There was the time McNutt had a contract to fly an old opossum trapper's gear into a hut on Nolan's Flat in the Perth River. Amongst his possessions were two crates of pullets, and I really believe those chooks took the helicopter to be some monstrous form of hawk, because they went literally mad during the flight in. By the time we landed they were so exhausted that they had become quiet, but their eyes were bulging like marbles from heads poked between the slates in their boxes. Bob Andrews, the trapper, told us later that those birds, which had been "in beaut laying form" before the flight, never laid another egg. Indeed, the sound of a passing aircraft was enough to send them into a frenzy during which they would dash into the bush and hide for several hours.

Mind you, chooks weren't the only helicopter fliers to go a bit crazy at times. Pilots also occasionally had strange bouts, doubtless brought on by too much time in the air. I was once with a pilot who claimed he could outmanoeuvre a wood pigeon, and put his theory into practice above the Balfour Glacier. It was a spectacular feat of aerobatics I would cheerfully have missed. Indeed, I did miss quite a lot of the performance because after the first series of tight circles and spirals in the helicopter I had the old eyes tightly closed. I think the pigeon won, but I'd be unwilling to argue the point.

When pilots became overtired they sometimes became subject to misjudgment, but there was little the shooter could do about it because the pilot was in control of the operation and, like a ship's captain, his word was law. If the decision he made involved danger it was possible to opt out, I suppose, but there was usually a bond of mateship which ruled this out especially after flying with the same pilot for a while. One of my more memorable experiences occurred while shooting tahr in the Perth Valley and flying the animals down to the riverbed opposite the Scone Creek hut for pickup. We had flown out quite a number of tahr and chamois, but with darkness coming on quickening feet there were still animals to gut and to get ready for the flight out. The machine arrived back and I put about half the remaining animals on the chain for what seemed likely to be the last flight of the day before darkness overtook us. I motioned to the pilot that I had the load attached and that he could move the machine away, but he climbed down and came back to tell me to put all the remaining animals on the chain.

I explained that some still needed gutting and that though daylight was disappearing fast I didn't think the machine could lift the full load. I saw the pilot's point, too: it would be disappointing to leave shot animals uncompleted . . . a sheer waste. However, the pilot was in no mood for discussion. He told me to "Put the bloody lot on the chain, and get into the machine". He then gunned her, but she simply would not lift the full load. Not to be outdone, he dragged the animals along the shingle riverbed until he was able to take off like a fixed-wing aircraft. If helicopters could speak that one would have been shouting loud and long. The vibration was something I would just as soon not have experienced, and I was, frankly, petrified with fear.

We gained about 200 feet in the run of a mile or so down the riverbed, but I just sat there in the vibrating machine expecting us to fall out of the sky at any moment. But we made it. Astonishing as it might seem, that over-loaded chopper managed to stagger to the depot. But it was a journey made at some cost! I wasn't surprised to learn that we had burned out a clutch and done in a major bearing. A very expensive last load, that one.

There has been a growing amount of criticism about helicopter operations, and some of it is doubtlessly justified. But I always like to recall the occasion when we were operating near the Paringa Bridge, flying out carcasses. We happened to be refuelling when a Land Rover swirled up and three bearded stalkers emerged, their jackets covered with insignia. We'd hardly had the opportunity to pass the time of day with them before they launched into a critical appraisal of helicopter operations as "criminal" . . . "an unspeakable despoliation of the nation's great natural heritage" . . . "exploiters of game which had been introduced by, and should be left for sportsmen".

This tirade went on and on for several minutes while I continued pumping fuel, and then the pilot tipped me the wink. It had happened before and he had a sure-fire method of discovering how true-blue his critics actually were.

He agreed there was a lot of good sense in what they claimed. And then he explained that as I would be busy for an hour weighing and loading the animals we had already brought out to the Paringa Bridge, perhaps one of them would like to take my rifle and place in the machine and try some shooting from the air? There was an immediate argument amongst the three of them as to which one should have this golden opportunity to take a flight. They were still arguing when we took off — after as rapid a change in idealism as I have ever seen.

But perhaps I should end this section with a story against myself —— for there were plenty of these. One of my shooting mates over quite a long period was a character named Ernie Wilson, a fellow with a fertile imagination and a persuasive way. Someone had given him an old lever-action model .44 and a great deal of ammo for it, but he hadn't yet had an opportunity to use it. After a very successful night spotlighting deer on Ferguson's Slip we had made about $500 and decided to invest this in helicopter time as a means of doubling our money quickly.

Instead of using my semi-automatic rifle, Ernie insisted that the helicopter expedition would be an ideal time to utilise the .44 and the free ammunition. According to Ernie the .44 was a weapon of hefty calibre that would poleaxe a bull. So we hired a machine, and I sat expectantly on the step with the .44 as the first sighting of deer came into range. It is my contention to this day that the first animal collapsed under the sheer weight of lead I pumped into it, and that the animals which followed at infrequent intervals must have suffered the same fate. Whether the shells rolled or whether it was the calibre of the bullets I simply don't know, but when we picked up the few animals which fell to that .44 we discovered that some of the bullets had penetrated a mere inch or so into the deer. Ernie never produced the .44 again, and it was a taboo subject on subsequent expeditions.

CHAPTER THREE

ANYTHING GOES — OR WENT

WHEN I FIRST began hunting on a semiprofessional basis, it was a case of just about "anything goes" as far as the handling of animals and payments for them were concerned. The venison industry has rather grown like Topsy, and officialdom wasn't always able to run fast enough to keep up with some of the characters operating over on the West Coast in those earlier days. The Coast had retained more of the frontier freedoms than the rest of New Zealand in more than the method of operating its hotels, and it tended to attract, as it still does, those of free spirit . . . the nonconformists.

Of course, conditions within the game meat recovery business have changed rather dramatically. There was much better control of hygiene, even before the new standards set by the West German Government, while the opportunities for earning big money from selling deer carcases without having to pay tax on the income have all but gone now.

There have been some howls of anguish from stalkers about the new system of game-animal payments by which a tax deduction is made at the time of sale and cannot be reclaimed until the annual return of income tax is filed. "Like, it's unfair," one old rogue told me. "It's as though they don't trust us."

And "they" do not. The old system of payment was, to many, little more than a lark, open to all manner of abuse. The shooter was required to furnish his name when selling game to an agent, and this led to the extensive use of aliases, with some emphasis being given to the use of names very similar to those of wellknown parliamentary characters, or of farmers known to oppose shooting on their properties, particularly if the animals had been poached from their land.

Inland Revenue must have suffered some disbelief when reviewing agents' returns to see the names of people such as Keith Holyoake, Rob Muldoon or Paddy Blanchfield popping up as deer shooters all over the West Coast — or of the farmer whose tax returns showed no signs of the 100 or so deer sold in his name. Local police constables, and even other hunters thought to have poached, had their names used indiscriminately in these returns designed to diddle the taxman.

There were certain frustrations when hunting for profit — indeed, for a living — when others muscled-in on good blocks. Old logging tracks were often valuable access routes and had to be kept secret if deer were located along them, for sitting on the roof of a car or van in a roughly constructed frame, with a powerful light and

One of our base huts on Kea Flat in the Landsborough, complete with chimney and other home comforts.

Inside the Top Hut in the Karangarua Valley. No evidence of a woman's hand here!

Meat-hunting in the Otoko River area showing venison hanging outside Reynolds Flat hut waiting for the meat collection plane.

a 'scoped rifle, could provide a generous return from a night's work. Opposition hunters were not welcomed in these circumstances.

Ernie Wilson and I had a period of spotlighting and suffered with poor grace the bugbear of others moving into our block. These fellows came wheeling into our area, emulating our own system and spoiling a block giving very worthwhile returns. However, we felt we were up to fighting fire with fire, and evolved a wonderful spoiling system.

Iridescent metal strips (like those used as reflectors on road marking-posts) which lit up when lights were turned upon them, were obtained and cut into teardrop shapes to resemble animal eyes. We erected these some distance in from the logging roads through swamp, gorse and fallen trees in our blocks. We might nail them to a tree perhaps a couple of hundred yards off the road, ensuring that a few leafy branches were between the set of "eyes" and the logging track. We set them up at least 150 yards in to make the "deer object" appear lifelike, and foliage added to the deception.

Operating with a spotlight and viewed through the 'scope of a rifle the screen was simple but effective. We practised the deception only in areas where there were no farm animals, while the reflector "eyes" were the same colour as those of game and did not blink — usual for deer looking into a spotlight — so they made a prime target.

We set up seven of these traps, and in four weeks five of them were surrounded with bullet holes. We often pondered over the reaction of the frustrated shooters who, after using a magazine of ammunition and then clambering through the gorse and swamp, found only a pair of metal strips. The advantage of the system was that once a shooter had loosed off a volley of shots at these targets any deer in the vicinity would have taken to their heels and would hopefully, come back on other days when the official block "owners" were the hunters.

Poaching takes many forms, of course, and I have been as guilty as the next fellow of an occasional fall from grace. For the foot shooter it can be a very cold business, requiring considerable patience and a deep cunning. The chaps I knew who poached, and the farmers whose land they poached on, usually had one thing in common: they were all shooters. More often than not the farmers closed their land to game shooting not so much because of the danger to stock but as a means of eliminating the shooting opposition.

The brother of a friend of mine took over the management of a farm property some ten miles south of Ross, a chap named Bruce Robinson, who was a keen hunter. He closed off his land to shooting, and this meant that I had to detour a considerable distance to arrive at the edge of swampland and cultivated ground, planted mainly in turnips, which adjoined it. Sitting in the gorse or on a clump of raupo I used to wait patiently for a deer to jump the fence and begin feeding. One shot was all I could afford, as the lights of the farmhouse would flash on and the farmer's Land Rover would come patrolling up and down the road with a spotlight sweeping the paddocks. After another hour or so I would sneak out and drag the deer from the paddock and into cover where I could gut it by torchlight.

The last time I visited Ross I was at a party with Bruce who told me: "You know, Harker, I had a 100 per cent suspicion it was you when I found the head and legs of a stag tucked away out there, but I never knew how you went about it."

And while delving back into my memories of the "bad" old days, I recalled just how serious blowflies — the conventional egg-laying fly and the "live maggot" blower — had been as a problem for the foot shooter who relied on some form of air transport to get his catch out every two or three days.

In remote areas which are shot on rare occasions there are usually no temporary meatsafes built, and the problem of keeping those persistent maggots off game meat is awkward - as bad today, I presume, as it was when I was ground shooting myself. I know that until about 1971 it was common enough practice for shooters to use those aerosol-type fly sprays at fairly frequent intervals, both directly into the open cavities after gutting and around the bullet holes. I have no doubt the taste of the meat suffered and could only hope that it was heavily spiced when served on the Continent. It was accepted that one large aerosol "bomb" was good for about six animals, depending always on how bad the fly problem was.

It is appalling to look back now on the sort of things which professional shooters accepted as normal only a few years ago. I recall summer work with a 7am start and a 6pm finish with animal carcases lying exposed most of the day. If the hocks hadn't been cut from those carcases they would have been able to "walk away" on their own with the help of the flies.

When Barry Petrie and I were hunting in Architects Creek we were using a tentlike collapsible meatsafe loaned to us by Goodwin McNutt. It had a fine mesh top and two of the four sides were mesh, and though we had it expertly staked down and soil piled on the bottom flanges, we still had problems with maggots inside the safe. Barry solved the mystery during a lengthy vigil when he saw blowflies settling on the roof mesh and dropping their eggs on to the deer inside.

There was the occasion, as well, when we were sitting on a riverbed airstrip quite a way up the Arawata watching animals shot from a helicopter being loaded into a Cessna 180. About half a dozen deer carcases lay near the plane as the pilot tipped fuel into the craft from jerrycans. When the tank overflowed, some of those animals were doused in av-gas (aviation fuel), but they were later loaded into the aircraft and flown out with the others!

Goodness knows what the gourmets thought of pyrethrum-flavoured patties or av-gas-tasting sausage, for there were some really disgraceful decisions made on the quality of some game in the years before proper (or perhaps better) control measures were instituted. The problem was that some agents were known by shooters to be lenient about the acceptable standards for meat, while others like Russ Douglas and Percy Singer, at Ross, Tony Condon, at Paringa, Tex Cain at Kaniere and others of their stripe, fulfilled their obligations to their employers and to the ultimate customers for the meat by rejecting the "rough stuff".

Considering what has occurred recently within the industry, with West

Building an airstrip in the Upper Waitoto Valley. Depressions were filled with logs and covered with soil to provide a usable surface for landing.

Howard Smith dropped in to collect our meat off a riverbed strip in the head of the Cascade Valley.

Home is where you hang your hat: living in a meatsafe on Toi Toi Flat, up the Landsborough Valley.

Germany's demands for higher hygiene requirements at game processing factories, it was just as well that there were honest men in the business in those earlier years or the multi-million dollar industry could have been stopped in its tracks early on, like a deer hit in the heart by a .308.

In the years when professional deer shooting was still climbing out of its infancy, many of those in the embryo industry were there for the adventure as much as the money. They were, many of them, weekend hunters who saw in the price of a carcase the opportunity to do all the time what the necessity to earn a living had allowed them to do only at weekends or during holidays. So the blokes humping a pack and rifle in some of the remote areas of the Coast, and getting their game kills out as best they could, might turn out to be skilled motor mechanics, builders, clerks — or plain layabouts. It was a marvellously free life at which one could work only as hard as necessity required. Some hunters were driven, as they had probably been in the jobs they had given up to do it, to make money and do well; others had the desire to hunt, but not the physique or the skills, and didn't last long at it; and others did what they had to do only when they had to do it.

Of these three general categories I guess I fitted the third more than the others, but it is not really an accurate description of my life, except for brief periods. There were times when I was fully engaged in hunting; times when I was deeply immersed in mapping and track blazing or clearing, and there were other occasions when I was taken up with the commercial aspects of the business, be it helicopter shooting, live-game capture, safaris or the like. Yet in retrospect some of the hunting I enjoyed most was the sort of thing I used to do with Ernie Wilson, with whom I had a pretty successful partnership and with whom, at odd times, I made a lot of money.

Ernie was a jovial companion whatever the conditions, whatever the returns. He was a character, a bloke with a vivid imagination and a retentive memory, with whom it was quite impossible to spend a dull hour. Although I was never greatly struck on spotlighting deer, I did quite a bit of it with Ernie because so many laughs were involved. In 1971 I approached Jim Ferguson, a farmer up the Waitaha, for permission to shoot a giant slip on his property. It was about half a mile wide at the mouth and went well back into the mountains. Better, it was the place where deer came out at night, and Jim Ferguson allowed me to shoot there provided I accepted responsibility for any stock shot. So Ernie and I, armed with sole permission to shoot the slip, moved in and began taking five or six animals a night off it, spotlighting. The shooting returns were so good, in fact, that we became blase about the whole business. We used to stroll across the slip with our spotlight, pick out a pair of eyes, and then casually sit down for a smoke while working out a plan of attack.

But shooting the deer, and there were some big fellows, was the easiest part of the business. Getting the carcases out was something else again. We had first to get them down the slip to the river, where we utilised truck or tractor tubes to float them downstream to an area where we could get a wheeled vehicle in. Jim Ferguson loaned us his front-end loader which removed a lot of deer - and a lot of heavy

Barry Petrie up the Cascade River bringing a young hind back to camp, also a rough 12-pointer stag's head.

Footshooting for venison in the head of the Karangarua, using the rifle sight as a telescope. On this particular day the author bagged twelve deer and six chamois.

work. At other times and in other places, however, the work was often tough, strenuous and prolonged, and it was in such circumstances that Ernie's ideas to utilise barrage balloons with trailing strops, or mechanical gadgets which seemed to owe as much to Heath Robinson as Jules Verne, bubbled to the surface to relieve the occasion of some of its gloom.

Once I was committed to professional hunting and had moved to Ross with my wife and young family, the need to work to pay the grocer, keep the car running and Santa Claus coming regularly every Christmas became increasingly important, yet with Ernie around it never became a chore. Sometimes it was as unplanned as the evening in November four years ago when Ernie was sitting with me on the front fence at Ross smoking and reminiscing. We had completed the dishes, so our standing with my wife Julie was A-ok.

"Let's take the light and have a quick crack down by the river," Ernie suggested. "Just an hour or so . . ."

Ernie's spotlight battery had been charged, he had been enjoying a very successful hunting period, and he felt in such deadly form that he suggested there was no need for me to bring a rifle. As the area he intended to spotlight was riverbed bordered with grassy flats I didn't bother to change my carpet slippers for stronger footwear. After all, Ernie was so positive, "the deer are that tame even a tele. sight won't be needed."

The evening was perfect . . . a steady wind blowing downstream . . . no moon to spoil the effect of the spotlight. We began to stroll in the very best of spirits. As darkness fell we were sitting on a boulder beneath a high bank looking back down the valley to where farmhouse lights twinkled. At our feet were hoofprints showing that two hinds had passed, and not so long before either. Even though their heading was away from the direction we were taking, the signs were encouraging. As we chatted and waited, I took a closer look at Ernie's rifle, surely a claimant for a gold medal as "prize relic of the year". The most prominent defects were a cracked stock, the lack of a 'scope, and a rear sight that fell either forward or back depending on how the weapon was shaken. The fact that it was a .270 calibre seemed the most likely reason why the bullet was able to fight its way down the barrel through the rust. I really was not surprised. Such things were part and parcel of Ernie Wilson. New or well-cared-for weapons, cars, or whatever, never had much appeal for Ernie.

But to work. Climbing up the bank we moved to the edge of a large sandy beach scoured by the river. I switched the light on and swept the powerful beam around the spit. At the far end of the area a pair of eyes reflected the light, which I quickly doused. We crept forward in the darkness until, suddenly, we stepped into the river. It was uncomfortable in carpet slippers, I can tell you. We climbed out, switched on the light and there, feeding with seeming unconcern, were our deer. Ernie wanted to whip off a shot there and then, but remembering the condition of his weapon I suggested we edge a bit closer. Each time he said, "Now", I urged him forward until we came to a slight knoll.

"Hell's bells, man, we must be almost on top of the damn thing," Ernie muttered.

He was right. I switched on the light and directly in front of us stood a hind peering into the powerful light. Ernie struggled to get a shell into the breech just as the hind began to move away. He pulled the trigger and the bullet must have passed just under her neck, for she was able to turn and gallop up the bank towards the safety of the bush. The next shot splattered a shower of fern leaves in front of her, so she turned along the bush edge.

I was almost doubled over laughing at Ernie's antics with the rifle. He really had to struggle to get each cartridge in and out, and by the time he had it loaded a third time the deer was just a memory. Ernie pressed the rifle into my hands with the advice to have a bash "or throw the bloody thing in the river". He was given to quick decisions of this type. So with Ernie toting the battery and light, I took station a pace or two behind, heavily armed!

By this time he was in no mood to waste time. He paced along at a regular clip, the light playing on the ground immediately in front of him and requiring that I remain close up to catch its benefit or take my chances with the rough ground surface. We were pushing our way through a network of fern when his excited mumble gave the clue: two deer walked up a steep bank about a chain or so ahead.

The first cartridge went into the breech with little pressure, and I was able to shoot the nearest deer as she turned. But the empty shell would not eject. I dropped the rifle and belted the bolt savagely. It slid back — leaving the case sitting in the breech. I grabbed the rifle and bashed it on the ground as Ernie shouted a warning. The deer had picked herself up and was charging straight towards us.

Meat recovery by packhorse in the Waitoto River area.

Grabbing the rifle by the barrel I swung it like a club and ran at the deer, which angled off as she neared us. I was flat stick, but lost sight of her as she got out of the orbit of Ernie's light, until he was able to find us again and illuminate the scene. It became a debate in my mind whether to try to club the deer or reach for the knife. A more rational and objective review of the situation would have told me that either was a waste of time, and that I was more likely to suffer injury than the deer would. However, a tangle of vines did what I was unable to do . . . it brought the hind down long enough for me to load and finish her off.

By this time I was feeling the effects of wearing carpet slippers and of my strenuous exertions chasing the hind; but Ernie had his blood up and wanted more deer. He suggested a run to the end of the flat in case any deer had been scared out of the centre clearings by the rifle shots. Stumbling along as best we could, we came to a pile of logs, and while resting flashed the light out on to the river to see two deer standing out in the open on a shingle beach. When I loaded and whipped the rifle up to my shoulder I discovered the back sight had fallen sideways and only the front sight remained intact. Despite a couple of well spaced shots, the deer jumped into the river and swam safely to the far bank. So it was back to find the animal we had shot. Being so far up the river we cut the large hind in two so that we could take turns with the burden, plus the slinky. I put this in my shirt and tied the sleeves in a manner which resembled a pack, and hung the front legs of the hind over my shoulders. I then lifted the heavy hindquarters on to Ernie's back for the walk out.

We swapped the burdens at intervals to share the strain until we gained the spot by the boulder where we had stopped for our first cigarette. Ernie put the light on and flashed it across the river to the far bank. A few hundred yards downstream stood a stag ready to wade out to cross below a very fast rapid. We shouldered our venison and stumbled down to where he would emerge from the river, but when we got there, the stag seemed to be almost the same distance down river, still intent on his crossing. The wily old fellow kept it up as long as we were able to do so, always seeming to be as far away at each outlet as he was before we started after him, until we were at the stage of dropping. In the end it was his night: we collapsed exhausted. And one of my carpet slippers was worn right through.

It was a couple of weeks later, with Christmas 1971 approaching, that my wife let it be known that she expected a stereogram to arrive in the front room before the festive season began. I began to feel a bit like a gun for hire as I took every job and opportunity that came along in an effort not only to provide the recordplayer, but to pay for a new rifle I had ordered without reference to the bookkeeper!

First there was Ernie suggesting some spotlighting -- with boots this time. The calendar showed a full moon due — it did not appear very strongly as the sky was clouded — and the valley was stroked by a warm breeze as we drove up as far as our wheels could take us before unloading the rifles and light, the battery for which was carried in a knapsack. We walked for half an hour or so until we came to a shingle fan. Ernie shone the light around and two sets of eyes lit up like miniature neon signs. With the light quickly doused we began to work our way as quietly as maybe over the loose shingle. We made about 120 yards, rested and tried the light again to find, surprisingly, the two stags standing a mere 50 yards or so to our right. Resting the rifle on Ernie's shoulder I shot one of the stags, and as the closer of the two turned to run it was simple enough to bowl him over as well.

After gutting these two we carried on to a small creek where the smell of deer grew very strong. We crawled forward, peering through fern and bracken. The moon became so bright and the night so clear that we could see 30 feet or so, yet there were no deer. We crawled on to the very edge of the river, and when Ernie flashed the light upstream two pairs of eyes lit up, almost as a welcoming sign. So it was forward again on hands and knees until we were able to stand in cover and flash the light again. Two hinds stood at the water's edge, but even as I rested the rifle on Ernie's shoulder they were bounding for the bush. The wind had swung round and blown our scent to them, and they needed no second warning.

The first hind reached the bush with bullets whistling round her rump, but the second was out of luck and crashed into the water. However, she too vanished in the rapids. So it was back to our gutted stags, where Ernie shone the light and was surprised to see a pair of eyes peering at us from behind a tree. With dead branches and foliage hanging down, we were unable to determine the animal's sex, nor could we get a clear shot. So we crawled up the creek bed until we were about 30 yards away from the lone tree. When the light flashed on, it caught a stag with a mouthful of leaves.

Ernie Wilson with tractor and trailer on Robinsons Slip is collecting our carcases the easy way.

Bringing chamois back to the Bonar Flat hut after an early morning shot up-river.

Poor old Ernie's ears must have been ringing like a peal of cathedral bells by now, but he generously allowed me to rest the rifle over his shoulder once more and the stag joined his two companions. By the time we humped the three stags back to the car and returned to Ross it was 4.30am.

With the cheque safely in our pockets we thought the clever thing to do was to invest it in helicopter time, remembering both the stereo and the new rifle, and thus double it more quickly. So at 5am. on the Saturday we were airborne at $3 a minute, and soon in luck. A stag burst from cover followed by several hinds as we flew over a saddle, and the whole operation was finished in a few minutes. But cloud drifted in to defeat the pickup and we had to wait for the weather to clear. We finished gutting, and between thunder and showers managed to slip back to the coast well satisfied with a useful return. On Sunday during a call at Fox Glacier I was asked to help Goodwin McNutt with chamois capture at the head of the Balfour River. We met with a big buck chamois determined not to be an export to the United States, and as I leapt from the helicopter step he turned and almost took me on the tips of his needle-sharp horns. Caught on the hop, I sidestepped and let him go past at the gallop. However, the next buck came easy and was followed by a family group which completed the load. We flew back to Fox Glacier, and as I drove home to Ross my eyes were mere slits from lack of sleep.

I was still soaking in the bath trying to ease the aches and pains when the telephone rang. Goodwin McNutt had two Americans who wanted to go hunting and needed a guide. Was I available? With the stereo and the rifle very much in my mind of course I was available, but the shriek of the alarm was sheer agony a few hours later. The Americans arrived and I drove them to the Whataroa in time to meet the chopper and the arrival of daylight.

Californian Gene Brush shot a big bull tahr with horns that measured 13¾ inches (349.25mm) and was unlucky not to get a large buck chamois which sprinted past us as we waited in hiding for another mob moving across the valley floor below us. William Sanders, another Californian, shot a good bull tahr which tumbled into a crevasse on a glacier and foiled our attempts to recover it, but he was later rewarded with a chamois above the usual standard, and the two returned happy with their hunt.

All this occurred within the space of a very few days, and illustrates my earlier point that the work and the money were available for those who wanted it. Certainly, everyone did not have the same opportunities perhaps of helicopter employment, but this, too, was something one had to work at, and to be available when needed on demand.

It was a tough time, but there was music at Christmas and no one complained when Santa Claus also brought me a new rifle,

CHAPTER FOUR

THE OLD FIRM

DURING MY YEARS on the West Coast as a hunter, guide and member of various commercial meat-recovery teams, the occasions I recall with most pleasure were those involving the team-mates I knew best. It was with such people that we could mount major expeditions in the sure knowledge of how much each man could handle, be it the weight of his pack, the length of a day's tramp, the height of a climb, or the skill of a stalk. Well rated amongst the top group of hunting companions were Barry Petrie, Peter Billington and Paul Bevernage. They were men for the tough haul or the tricky climb, good companions always.

Thus it was no surprise that we should have found ourselves, early in 1969, on our way to explore, map, and hunt the seldom-visited region between Sawtooth Ridge and McKenzie Col surrounding the headwaters of the Big Waitaha River. We had learned that a track had been blazed in 1951 from the farming settlement on the south side of the Waitaha to the County Stream (about two-thirds of the way up the Valley), and the lower reaches included popular hunting areas that I had covered and later tramped many times, up from Whirling Water to Mt Neville, Bartrum Creek and the Kiwi Flats, and Moonbeam Torrent. But further on, the country did not get many visitors. Indeed, from Whirling Water onwards, the track became less and less apparent and soon proved to be overgrown and completely to have disappeared.

The party included an American, Tommy Wilder, and we started at daybreak because there was a lot of walking to do — although we didn't fully realise at that stage that we were in for a tough three days of crashing through the thick mat of jungle which lay mile upon mile along the river's edge until we reached the snowgrass and moraine highlands. Progress was fine at the beginning, but the forest produced some surprises to test our resilience and our tempers. There were the barriers of windfalls, and then the huge slips that occasionally forced a detour, or a climb over a height of around 300 feet. These rapid ascents tended to burn up energy.

The route was cut in places by natural water-races, and these guts required careful skirting, as Paul Bevernage was to learn. We were negotiating one of them when he gave a sudden shout of warning. The ground had collapsed beneath his weight, and he had toppled forward towards the deep rock gut. Burdened with pack and rifle he was without much manoeuvring capacity as he slid forward, but by sheer good luck he grabbed hold of a piece of fern and hung on grimly, with his back to the shale bank. Pete Billington moved in like a rocket to help him from above, while I dropped my pack and climbed into the gut to get beneath him. While Pete held him from above, I crawled up until I was able to anchor my feet and reach up to grasp Paul's dangling ankles. Once he was able to lower on to my shoulder, the risk was over, and we climbed out of the gut and back on the track.

Moonbeam Torrent provided the first real opportunity for a rest, and this came after we had been on the move for nine hours. A snack of cheese and dates and the ever-welcome smoke gave us a chance to recharge the energies for what still lay ahead. Moonbeam Torrent, which begins in the Yandoit Glacier, can live up to its name and provide precarious crossings, but we used to utilise the trunk of a huge totara which had fallen across the water about 120 yards up from the confluence. Our own feeling on that trip was that the journey to Moonbeam was the easy part, and that the drag up the almost vertical bush climbs and rounded granite boulders that seemed to bank one on another was heartbreaking - and lungbursting.

By the time we got to the County Stream we were all but done in. Considering that we had accomplished a two-day trip in thirteen hours it was something of an accomplishment nevertheless, and Barry really made our day by discovering an overhanging boulder which provided a dry camp. There was no argument from any of the party. The sleeping bags were unrolled and we slept to the whisper of the nervous treetops.

There had been mist during the night, but a change in the wind took it rapidly away to leave a cloudless sky and a dew-drenched landscape. From below came the sounds of the turbulent County Stream, a foaming barrier to our further progress, so we discussed a crossing as we fed ourselves sugared dates for instant energy.

Less than 400 yards upstream from where the County joins the Waitaha there is a shingle slide rising some 20 to 25 yards from the water's edge, while at its base is a mighty boulder which appears to overhang the water. This is an illusion. We found

Crossing between Sawtooth Ridge and Mt Hitchen, a part of the route now shown on Lands & Survey maps as Harker Pass.

a climb to the top of the slip easy enough, for the shingle was well settled, and on the top uphill side there was a windfall which we blazed to indicate the start of the track we intended to establish. It wound along a series of stony bluffs until reaching a very old campsite. Ten paces past the campsite a narrow wash dipped steeply to the County Stream bank, and it was down there that we forced a passage.

The river was at its crescendo at this point, and put up a fine, misty spray as we prepared to cross. The water was deep and moving at speed. I left my pack and rifle and began the leap from boulder to boulder, with my tricounies grasping for traction on the smooth surfaces. The last big boulder was a couple of yards from the far bank which was, in its turn, covered with a brownish slime. The water was roaring through in a white rage at this point, so I gave a mental "one-two-three-and-away", flinging myself forward and gripping at the slime-covered bank like an octopus.

Mine was the easiest part, really. My mates had then to take a boulder apiece from bank to bank and fire the packs and rifles from hand to hand, rather like loading meat carcases on the wharf in the days before mechanical methods replaced slings — only much, much tougher. Just imagine balancing precariously on a boulder in the middle of a foaming river, with a steel-framed pack flying at you. Catch, re-anchor ready to heave the fifty or so pounds on, and then turn to catch the next one. Chain gang . . . As I watched the exercise I wondered whether I'd be able to collect on my all-risks policy if the circumstances were described to the insurance company.

When it came time for the lads to make their final leap, I cut a branch and stationed myself downstream ready to offer a helping stick to any who missed his flip, but they made it with the skill of a Russian gymnastic troupe.

The marvellous feelings of accomplishment in the mountains don't, as a rule, give the hunter much time to dwell on them, for he's faced almost immediately with the next test. Once we were gathered on the south bank we had immediately to plan a climb up on to the spur leading to the Blomfield Range. We were intent on making a good track for those who might follow, so we carefully forced a way through the thick mat of undergrowth. Paul was of immense value in this: being the smallest, he was able to go ahead and look for the easiest routes. It also meant he had to be the fittest, because he was covering more ground. Barry and I trod along behind, clearing the bracken which Tommy and Peter had uprooted.

We followed the long ridge to the alpine scrub, and though it was open and easy walking, there was no actual indication of position. It was noticeable as we began to circle south around the Blomfield Range that the bush growth changed: stunted vegetation, due to heavy snowfalls, gave way to belts of leatherwood, turpentine, and senecio which made for easy walking; far below we glimpsed the Waitaha and an area of open tussock. This led us to making a major "blue".

We decided to descend to the tussock area, as we must have passed the mighty Waitaha Gorge, and to drop down into the river to boulder-hop the rest of the way upstream. So it was down to the riverbed, and a particularly beautiful part of it at

Good companions. *Left to right:* Peter Harker, Alan Weir, Barry Petrie and Paul Bevernage, a photograph taken after travelling through the Whitcombe Pass following two weeks' shooting in the Whitcombe and Wilkinson River areas.

Ballance Lake at the head of the Waitaha. This lake bears a name suggested by the author to the Lands & Survey Department.

The headwaters of the Waitaha taken during the summer months on our first exploration.

that. There were mountain daisies and white fuchsia and a waterfall — ideal for the scenic enthusiast with a colour film.

But we found scaling the sides of the gigantic boulders which formed the path of the main river was a considerable feat and a heavy charge against physical energy as the day faded. A newly erected Forestry Service hut was available on the south side of the Waitaha some 750 yards before the confluence with Reid Creek. The best route, we discovered, lay on the north bank and I spent a considerable time with Paul and Barry making large stone pyramids to mark this route.

While the south bank involved a lot of scrub work and detours, the north bank, being the "cold" side, was mostly shale and progress was definitely faster. And the hut was ideal: a six-man unit with kerosene cooking facilities because of the lack of firing for an open fireplace. As we lay in the sleeping bags that night we heard animals feeding outside, and later investigation of the hoofprints showed it had been chamois.

The group was awake and away early. Indeed, Barry, Paul and I were treading our way through the tall spanish grass to the edge of the Waitaha by the time the sun had the surrounding snowcapped peaks a glowing pink turning slowly to a soft gold. This far back in the mountains meant that the swift-flowing river was a mere 15 yards across, but it having begun and filtered through at least five glaciers on its two-mile journey to where we stood meant that we were far from eager to dash across it. But we made it, scaring a family of mountain ducks in the process, and within five minutes of leaving the hut both Barry and Paul had shot a chamois apiece, and I had some grand pictures of an old buck.

The first small glacier just past Dean Canyon provided some cat-and-mouse shooting, for we had no sooner put foot on the tail of a steep frozen snow shute when a small herd of deer appeared well above us. Through the 'scopes it looked as though they had virtually committed suicide, as the pocket into which they ambled seemed to be sealed. Barry led the chase at a gutbusting pace, passing up an easy shot at a chamois in pursuit of our evening meal. Having to rely on what the mountains provided for eight days meant that the chance of venison could not be lightly passed over.

As the three of us pussyfooted round the last bend, rifles at the ready, we could almost smell those venison steaks frying in the pan. We were in for a sad disappointment. Round the bend there was a clear view of mountains — but no deer. Yet the animals had hardly been out of our sight, and there was no indication of where they could have gone.

We simply had to swallow our disappointment in the absence of venison steaks and carry on, following the lower spur of Sawtooth Ridge until early afternoon, with stops only for shooting and filming. Circling back to the edge of Ballance Lake we had a wonderful time skiing down a steep section of the mountainside, flanked by icefields. We traversed the spur between two lakes and ambled down through the snowdrifts to the valley floor. We had begun the drop to a series of tarns when,

This stag leapt from the top of a vertical waterfall and landed in the pool below. Taken in the head of the Waitaha.

Descending from the Katzenback Ridge near the Wilkinson River region, Peter Billington seeks a shot and a suntan.

from a fault directly below us, a hind, followed quickly by a buff-coloured stag, hove into view. Caught unawares and on a part of the terrain without good footholds, we scattered to take up good firing positions.

Paul reached the ledge first, but his shots went wide. Barry was busy turning the air "blue" because of bullet-feed problems, and by the time I'd got into a comfortable firing position the two deer were about 275 yards away and moving. At full gallop over rough ground they proved a tricky target, but my chance came when the stag topped a rounded knoll.

Give the (expletive deleted) another one," yelled Barry, the demands of his stomach overcoming all else in the excitement of that moment as the stag jerked with the impact of the bullet. The advice was well meant, but difficult to follow, for even though wounded the stag was by now about 450 yards away.

Steadying the rifle on the rock, I wound the 'scope up to 9-power and took a very careful bead before squeezing gently. At that moment I could have hugged my old buddy Vic Eckhoff, who carried out my fine optic adjustments. The stag came to a halt on the edge of a waterfall and there was a loud, "Whoopee", from Paul as the animal tumbled over the edge and down into the water far below.

Weighed down with steaks and haunches, we proved a welcome arrival back at the hut that night, and before long the sound of sizzling steaks joined the crackle of the transistor.

We spent the next few days gaining details for our wall map, which we left at the hut to assist those who followed, and doing a stalk to keep hand and eye in tune. Paul and Barry had never shot tahr until this trip, but they got their opportunity one morning as we lay on a high ridge overlooking the tail of the McKenzie Glacier. While using the glasses I noticed a rust-coloured bull tahr feeding on a narrow razorback about 750 yards away. My two mates drew straws as I mentally worked out a stalk that would bring us to within reasonable shooting range, so we began by working our way up the centre of the glacier until we reached a narrow gut slicing down the glacier-bed wall.

Without ice axes we had to use extreme caution, for the likelihood was that a slip would solve any old-age problems that might be ahead of us. As we gained height, the teeth of our tricounies could just find chinks in which to bite, and it was a considerable relief to top that gut. Paul had drawn the short straw, so Barry and I watched him cart his 30-06 down towards the bull feeding on the clump of tussock. He set himself and fired two shots. Both missed, and the tahr was off and away across the mountain.

I dropped my camera and grabbed my Winchester as the old fellow rounded a bluff. I managed to pump a quick shot into him, and he fell into a water shute. An inspection showed he was indeed an ancient one, and by the appearance of his horns he had had some rugged experience.

Paul, wondering how he had missed, found his 'scope was "juicy fruited", so he uncoupled the mounts and reverted to open sights.

It was our experience then that the deer preferred the mountain slopes facing the top of the valley, especially around the Reid Creek area, while tahr were in the high south-west bluffs overlooking the Syme Lake, and chamois through the valley at higher altitudes.

During that night clouds swept low over the region and brought drizzle, but an early morning wind swept both away towards the sea. We had chosen to leave the headwaters of the Waitaha by a new route through a pass we believed would take us to the north side of Ragged Peak. So on leaving the hut we made our way downstream on the south bank until directly opposite Spanish Grass glacier, where we forded the river and began following the trail along the north bank - the one which Paul, Barry and I had established a few days earlier. We discovered our own rock pyramids a boon in saving the backtracking which would have become necessary had the way not been clearly marked. Indeed, it seemed no time before we reached the track through the Chainman's Creek, and followed the waterway north on to the newly-christened Winchester Flats.

These flats are not particularly extensive, but they are picturesque with lush grass and odd clumps of fuchsia and mountain berry along the bushline. We headed up the centre creek, which gets most of its water from the spectacular Michele Waterfall, and kept to the middle of the snowgrass spur which is at one spot divided by a near-vertical shingle slide. This required a very cautious descent to the winter glacier bed at the lower southern side of the shingle fan. We followed the glacier up

Exploring Reid Creek at the head of the Waitaha.

Shooting chamois off the Seddon Col, an area very tricky to reach because of the amount of serious climbing involved.

American Tommy Walker collecting firewood around the campsite in the Hitchen Basin. Our cover was made from fern and bracken heaped over with snow tussock and branches laced with flax.

the mountain until a long, shale bed, very narrow, angled in from the right and led us to the snowgrass above.

This was the beginning of the pass — now shown as Harker Pass on Land and Survey Department maps — on which we had gambled as likely to make our route a reality. Instead of ploughing immediately through the scattered snowdrifts we scrambled up to a sheltered ledge to look back at the region, rugged and beautiful, which we had tramped over and shot for the previous week. It was awe-inspiring, in a way, that we had managed to cross all those glaciers, climbed those rough slopes and battled our way through all those miles of forest. There were areas, perhaps, where we had been the first to pass that way, and that added to the awe of it all.

After a rest we turned north and began to kick steps in the few remaining snowfields until, rounding a granite obstacle, I was able to shout the good news that ahead, with its peak nuzzling the mists, was Mt Hitchen and the south-east face of Mt Allen. This really topped off our day, and there was a flock of about thirty cheeky keas to add their greeting to our own noise. So it was down the east spur of the Hitchen Basin towards the top of Isobel Falls to a campsite I had earlier established, where we spent the night.

We weren't able to wallow in the pride of our success the next day, for a thick belt of fog engulfed the mountains and we were forced to grope our way down the face of Mt Allen to the last belt of forest, and then on to a farm some twenty miles from where we had left our vehicle at the start of the journey. An obliging farmer brought Paul's sister along with transport, so we completed a tough one in mobile comfort.

Note: In the early 1970's the Forest Service cut tracks and erected swing bridges up the valley, and a hut is available at Moonbeam Torrent.

Just a few weeks later Peter Billington, Paul and Barry joined me in another expedition hunting the top tributaries of the Whitcombe. We tramped in to the Neave Creek hut and decided to make that our headquarters for a few days until a couple of lads from Ashburton arrived via the Manuka Point-Cattle Creek route to join us.

While my mates took off down the Whitcombe the next day to build a log walkway, I headed up into the Whitcombe Pass to put up track markers so that our intended visitors would have a clue to how far and which way. As this job was finished with hours to spare, I made a dash up Mt Neave to look for game, though I was hardly dressed for playing around at the 5500 feet mark with shorts and a ragged bush singlet — wool, of course. The chamois I bopped up about that level was hardly compensation for the cold. Meanwhile, the lads had located a route over the spur which divided the Wilkinson and Whitcombe Rivers, and reported game in profusion.

We were abroad the next morning as the sun filtered off the Katzenbach Ridge, and intended to move tents and equipment across the Whitcombe, over the toe of the Katzenbach and on to the confluence of the Thorndike Creek and Wilkinson

River. This we accomplished, with time left for hunting. We left the campsite situated on the west side below the Thorndike Creek and boulder-hopped up a small creek and on to the base of a large moraine field. We clumped on to the base of the existing glacier and spread out to cover the region, with Barry and his .270 remaining to seal the game net at the edge of the moraine. While I moved right, Pete and Paul took the edge of the glacier with the idea of stalking around at a height well above the sloped glacier bed walls. The gut I followed cut me off from seeing the others, but there was sign everywhere of deer.

Suddenly the kaa-boooommmmm from Paul's .306 shattered the stillness, followed soon afterwards by the deeper roar of Pete's big-bore rifle. The noise had hardly stilled before Barry's .270 barked, and I thought that on the basis of those three shots there would be venison for dinner that night. I continued to climb towards the contoured summit, and a scramble of stones had me dancing on to a rocky outcrop to check. It was Paul, travelling across the mountain face at a decent clip, obviously on important business, so I decided to stay out of the way and enjoy a cigarette, I just managed to get it lit when the kaa-boooom came echoing down again, so I climbed up to the crest to assist. In a gut there was a pair of antlers sticking out of the tussock, and from where I stopped two really large stags could be seen against the skyline on an adjoining ridge. I had a look at them through the 'scope and made out 14 and 16 points respectively.

The return from less than ninety minutes' shooting had been so good that it looked as though the region would have us as guests for a few days. There was one disturbing factor, though: quite apart from the noise we were making, we noticed that every ten or fifteen minutes hundreds and hundreds of tons of ice would peel off Mt Evans and go crashing down the mountainside with a thunderous roar. This fantastic show, specially staged by Nature, went on with such monotony that it became commonplace, and after a time we tended to ignore it.

We decided that with so much meat available, Pete and I would take a supply of back steaks and a haunch or two back to our base camp at Neave Creek, then return to the Wilkinson at first light the next day, while Paul and Barry remained at the fly-camp for an evening shot.

We hadn't taken the weather into our calculations, and the next morning there was drizzle with the promise of a real downpour later. It was all speed to the fords, where I built a pile of stones on the west bank of the Wilkinson as a guide post, and then sloshed through with Pete to the tents. By this time it was raining heavily, so our companions decided to abandon the fly-camp and return to the Neave Creek hut. It took us perhaps fifteen minutes to break camp and get back to the ford, but within that time the river had risen and swept away the cairn I had built. We were fortunate indeed that we had made our decision so quickly, for it enabled us to get across the Wilkinson and the Whitcombe as the rain really poured out of the sky and the river rose to waist-deep level with dramatic speed. It was this weather which greeted my old hunting mate from the east side of the Alps, Alan Weir. He had been hunting the headwaters of the Havelock but, when he heard we intended to shoot

Syme Lake named by the author in the head of the Waitaha Valley, three days in from the coast.

the mountain tops between Kea Pass and Park Dome, he had sent a telegram stating that he'd join us down the Whitcombe. And so he had, with John Clinton as his young hunting partner for the trip.

Perhaps they brought us better weather, for the next morning the rain had passed, and the dark clouds began to clear from around Mt Neave, which Paul Bevernage and Pete Billington decided to shoot that day. Barry Petrie took John Clinton on a trek to the true left of Neave Creek, and Alan and I decided to try Whitcombe Pass, where he had seen thirteen hinds during his crossing and felt sure a huge stag had to be in close attendance. As we moved along the mountainside we used the glasses on every basin or pocket that might offer haven to the herd, but saw no game. Finally we dropped to the gravel leading to the crest of the pass, having virtually written off any chance of seeing deer. Alan was recalling a rude story about some Australian girls as we strolled along when a hind appeared on the skyline ahead of us, barking furiously.

I hastily flicked the lever action down on my Winchester, then changed my mind. Alan nodded, took careful aim, and produced the old Weir trick — one shot, one deer. When we got to the fallen animal we saw she lay almost exactly, to within a few inches, on the top of the pass, half in east and half in west. The sun was by this time on a sharp dive, and we calculated about an hour of daylight remained. We took the venison we required, and then decided that with the distance we had to cover back to the Neave hut there would be need for speed all the way.

We began with a sort of boulder-hopping jog, dancing from flat rock with giant strides to flat rock for the first few hundred yards, and then Alan struck one that tipped. He disappeared from in front of me virtually within a twinkling of an eye, accompanied by a scream that chilled my innards. I scrambled down to him, and within a minute his knee was swollen to twice its normal size and was giving him gyp. The sort of night temperatures in that region were such that there was no future in trying to stay out without proper shelter, so we had painfully to carry on down the rocky stream. He used me as a crutch, and in pitch blackness we inched our way back to camp. That square of light was so welcome I could have yelled had I the strength left when I sighted the illuminated window.

And for poor old Alan it was a damn sight worse, just how much no one quite realised until it was discovered later he had a broken kneecap. The pain that lad must have endured. . . And he missed hunting the headwaters of the Wilkinson and the chance of exploring the glaciers, being confined to camp until the water levels dropped to a fordable depth. Home it had eventually to be, but we wanted one more try, so we splashed across the Thorndike and remained on the west side of the Wilkinson until the river forked.

At the confluence of the Wilkinson and the west Katzenbach Stream, which originates from the east ice face of Mt Evans, we left the bank and headed in a gentle climb around the side of the cone, which proved a marvellous place for tahr. Large tussock-covered moraine fields flowed down from the ice and snowcapped ridges, while from the sheer rock faces of Evans a series of narrow ledges spiralled upwards to sunbathed ridges. The place gave every appearance of being a bull tahr paradise, but try as we might we did not manage to spot one. We tried one or two of the spurs, but there wasn't even new animal sign — until I saw, quite suddenly in front of me, a pair of antlers! Looking for tahr, and we found a stag. Barry was behind me carrying my Winchester, so I motioned to him that there were deer ahead, as a large group of hinds also hove into view from a basin above us, followed by a spiker and the kingpin stag. They ambled across the mountainside, getting a sharp hurryup from the stag from time to time.

Barry had first shot, and knocked the stag sideways — a beautifully clean kill. It was in splendid condition.

Meanwhile, the rest of them took to their heels down the nearest creek. But others began to appear from all over the place. First there was a spiker with two hinds scrambling out of a nearby basin, and then a mob of eighteen trotting through the valley proper. We didn't chase them, as the day was dying and the next morning, early, we would be on our way out. Alan and John had to leave first to get a decent start because of Alan's injured knee, and by the time Pete, Barry and Paul and myself started off the rain had turned to snow - and the temperature had plunged. Foul weather followed us all the way to the Whitcombe Pass, but it was sunshine down the Louper Pass to the Rakaia, where we bunked at the shepherd's hut at Cattle Creek.

It was there in the diary, dated 1945, a visiting doctor had written: "It is my personal observation that the Rakaia deer herd is on the decline. Been here three days and have seen but 200 deer . . ."

Our journey ended a few miles before the Jellicoe Hut where Alan had left his Land Rover at the start of his tramp over to the Neave hut. We would not have managed 200 deer, but we certainly had collected enough memories and stories about the Wilkinson and Whitcombe to burn down a few candles in hunting huts for years to come.

Note: Like the Waitaha, the Whitcombe Valley has now been well opened up.

CHAPTER FIVE

CLIMBING HIGH

CLIFF PEART was born at Gore during the depression years, so he learned early that anything you needed required a lot of hard work. As a youngster he worked with his father and brothers for gold, and later he tried shopkeeping in Christchurch. He was as generous in business as he later proved to be in the bush, but though it made for brisk sales, his generosity didn't produce much in the way of profit. So he tried his hand at building before finding his way to the West Coast where he shot the headwaters of the Arawata for a year, carrying the carcases down to Williamson Flats where they were flown out by fixed-wing aircraft.

In 1966 Cliff spent some time working with helicopters, but he found he preferred foot shooting, where he could be his own man, and so he looked around for a block to shoot. When the immortal Rod Rudolf stopped shooting the Waitoto River, Cliff took over; he recalls vividly the troubles he encountered in getting his horses through the bush to the open flats. With no tracks to speak of, he cursed the whole way in — to find when he got there that there was little grass on the extensive flats as deer had cropped them almost to a bowling-green finish.

For those latter-day visitors to the region whose eyebrows might already be raised, let me point out that Cliff and a mate, Kevin Bythell, counted a mob of 200 deer at the confluence of the Te Nahi and the Waitoto, and in one month he shot 87 stags without having to go into the bush. Some of these monsters weighed out at 300lbs (136 kilos) apiece.

But Cliff didn't just exploit the area. He cleared airstrips, built huts, cut miles of good, open tracks, and put walking wires across narrow river sections. During the early part of 1971 I spent quite a lot of time with him, along with Barry Petrie, exploring and climbing throughout the tributaries of the Waitoto, as well as assisting with meat-hunting.

It was in the Waitoto that Cliff provided me with the chance first to use horses to recover carcases. He was expert himself in handling horses, while I had difficulty in working out the head from the tail, and my experience of them had been limited to what I had watched in television Westerns. I gave him plenty of amusement by trying to mount from the wrong side, but if Cliff had seen the spectacular mistakes I made out of sight of his cabin when trying to load deer carcases, he'd have split his sides laughing.

Cliff Peart and friend in the Waitoto Valley. Cliff was one of the most popular personalities amongst meat-hunters in South Westland.

Another way of bringing a stag back to camp.

Five deer recovered from near the Drake River flats following a morning shoot.

However, shooting on this particular expedition was merely part of the excitement. I stayed overnight in the tiny Drake Flats hut which had the House Full sign up with two professional meat-hunters, and two trophy hunters from Dunedin eager to shoot the flats. A heavy frost had the stags roaring and gave promise of a magnificent day, clear and bright with a hard light. I decided to take the camera rather than a rifle and try for the open tops, though Cliff had warned me that the bush behind Drake Flats was heavily laced with boulders which made progress occasionally heartbreaking. Ahead though was Flanagan's Peak, and that was my objective.

The early part of the climb was reasonably open, and besides the increase in huge boulders there was a heavy underscrub which cut progress back to limping pace. And then the mountainside rose more steeply, with easier bush and a better spacing between the boulders. I had some luck, too, in stumbling on to a game trail which took me swiftly through the alpine scrub. A wall of rock swept steeply ahead and I could see that fringes of snow tussock showed at the highest point. I had no chance of making it up with my boots on, so I took them off and with my socks giving me greater grip on the tiny chinks and footholds I was able to inch my way up. Looking down had an upsetting effect on my stomach, so I kept my eyes strictly on the job at hand. Boots back on, I made my way along the slate rock ridges with groups of nine or ten chamois as my distant companions. By midday I was one peak off the western arete of Flanagan's Peak which stood magnificently alone at 7,500 ft (2886 metres). It was a challenge, but the day was so clear that I decided to pick up Nature's gauntlet — a decision I was to regret several times during that afternoon.

But the final reward was well worth the effort. The four peaks leading to Flanagan's lay below me, while away at the head of the Waitoto Valley Mt Aspiring, snowclad, commanded the region, By looking westward I could see down and above the Haast Range clear through to the Waipara and Arawata tops.

Looking north, the three watersheds of the Drake lay spread below me, and the icefields of the Sombrossy, Ohio, Pickelhaube and the Donald glaciers were in full view. There was a feeling up there of command, of the greatness and the sweep of Nature's power which I seemed briefly to share as I sat gazing at a creation beyond Man's technology. Up there it was easier to understand why people like to test themselves against mountains . . . but I had to be practical. I had to go back.

Following a razorback ridge on the Commissioner Range I climbed down to the Draughtsman Spur and sat on a rock abutment looking into a fine hanging basin, which I took to be part of the Donald River. It was tempting to stay longer, but there were clear signs from the sun that daylight was on the wane. For all the distance I had travelled, there had been no sighting of deer, although chamois were plentiful, some in full winter coat — it was April — while others still sported summer pelts. The latter tended to be females.

By the time I reached the alpine scrubline the sun was dropping quickly behind the Haast Range. The descent through the bush was hard work all the way and, strangely, deer started to appear in fairly numerous small groups. It had been a

Flannagans Peak, taken from the top of the main ridge leading to the south abutment.

Crossing an awkward section of the Waitoto.

wonderfully memorable day, and the carcases hanging in the meatsafe behind the hut suggested the boys had also, in their way, spent the day to advantage

Accompanied by Barry Petrie we made our way later to the grass flats opposite the Stormwater and Bonar Rivers where Cliff Peart had built a solid log cabin with sleeping compartments for six. He was shooting the area with Dave Rossiter, while Barry and I intended to shoot and photograph around the headwaters of the Waitoto. We kept to the edge of the river until we were almost opposite the Pearson River confluence, where the bush offered easy access. At the second big slip on the south bank we climbed high on to a bush plateau to follow a well-used game trail which led us to a beautiful tarn set in a clearing. There seemed to be deer everywhere, so while Barry stalked a stag I photographed reflections of the high north range in the calm water.

We climbed higher, chopped a course up an old creek bed and stepped out on to the open moraine fields below Mt Skyscraper. Below us was an ice-covered lake and, as we watched, a huge slab of ice dropped away from the mountainside and thundered into the muddy waters. We had reached the last high shelf of snow tussock, and while we sat in shelter behind a boulder munching chocolate there was a hollow booming followed by a series of crashes. Behind us an avalanche of snow and ice cascaded over the lip of a huge bluff.

We sat there aghast . . . and then there was a mad scatter. It was far too cold to look for game in the open alpine and moraine fields so we made our way back to the picturesque tarn, protected and warm, and lay down to thaw out. The enthusiastic

The "log cabin", Bonar Flat hut, in the Upper Waitoto — an outside view.

The interior of the Bonar Flat hut. The bunks might appear to lack that "inner-spring comfort" — and they did! The purpose of the wallpaper is not for decorative arrangement, but to keep the draughts out.

A chamois watches with interest as the author climbs a broken ridge above the Waitoto on his way to the snowfields.

Barry went off after his elusive stag while I decided to doze in the alpine sun. I was in a state halfway between waking and sleeping when I heard the distant roar. It was repeated, and as I came up towards full wakefulness I vaguely thought Barry was having his wee joke. Another roar; a half-hearted effort that no stag would bother to answer. And then I heard the *slurp, slurp, slurp* of someone moving through the water.

As I turned over I shouted to Barry: "Hell, mate, you've got a lot to learn about making deer noises . . ."

Standing knee-deep in the water regarding me was a 9-pointer stag. I continued to stare while reaching for my camera, trying to line the fellow up a mere twenty feet away. His antlers were covered with pieces of branches and some moss, and I had him nicely lined up when he snorted, turned, and charged off through the water. Fifteen minutes later Barry returned with a leg of venison.

On our way back to the river we saw two stags challenging each other's lordship over four hinds, the larger appearing to be of 10 or 11 points, while the other was obscured by bush. Although we crept noiselessly up to them, the wind spoiled our chances when a hind caught our scent and they scattered. However, it would have been an easy task to shoot the largest stag — easier than trying to photograph him, as I found when the film was developed. We had not gone far when a 6-pointer crashed out of the bush to stand about fifteen feet from us, followed by a huge hind which I managed to photograph as she stood and barked at us. We counted seventeen deer within a handy radius, all very quiet, suggesting they had not been subject to helicopter shooting, unlike those around the fringes of the headwaters' scrub.

It was during this expedition that Cliff suggested it was impossible to climb the front face of Mt Datamos, 6,000 feet (1830 metres) high and protected by its steep rock faces. It was the sort of challenge I was young enough and silly enough to accept, especially as I had already been studying the mountain with a possible climb in view. Cliff's idle remark was the clincher — and Barry Petrie was an eager companion. We crossed the Waitoto in an Indian-style canoe which nearly gave us an ice-cold ducking on several occasions before we fetched up on the south riverbank. It was while we were briskly making our way across the flats and into the boulder-filled shingle slip that we discovered we had no rope along. I had been so intent on getting the various lens changes for the camera that I had overlooked this important item.

As the terrain rose sharply, so did the temperature. The sun came up above the Drake Range and the heat began to be reflected intensely from the rocks, yet it seemed no time really before we were standing by the first sheer bluff. This we overcame with some serious climbing, and we took a break for smoko on a ledge.

Let me make it plain here and now that climbing Mt Datamos is not really for weekend trampers and stalkers. Barry and I had in our day-to-day hunting gained a lot of experience of rock climbing, but we were not experts.

The noises really did come from this stag, which took flight as the author reached for his camera.

The Indian-style canoe which started our climb to Mt Datamos and ended its days when an injured Barry Petrie put both feet through the bottom of it.

    We resumed our ascent on the next rock wall, and with hairline cracks to provide grip we inched our way up to yet another ledge which provided a cramped and rather precarious resting place. The abutment we then followed turned out to be a deadend, and we had to climb down 50 feet to a cleft in a bluff which gave us access to a good ridge.

    Barry began to descend when, totally without warning, he slipped and lost his grip on the smooth rock. He disappeared quickly from sight but less quickly from earshot, for I heard a couple of muffled thuds as he hit ledges on which we had previously gained a respite during our climb.

    Than all was silent, except for the rattle of a dislodged stone. I stood in shock.

    But action was called for in this situation. I edged to the side of the rock wall and peered over. Well below I could see Barry wedged in a shallow recess, lying on his back. Below him again, had he continued his fall, was a drop of another 40 feet on to jagged rock.

    The descent was actually made in record time, yet it felt like an age while I was finding my way down to where he lay. An arm sprawled straight out. His legs were bleeding and there was a thigh cut and marks which suggested eye-catching bruises were on the way. But Barry was a hard fellow to keep down. I knew he must be all right as the cursing increased in tempo, and he gradually managed to struggle into a sitting position. I gabbled a load of old rubbish; for both of us it was a reaction to shock. We spent an hour just talking, until our nervous systems seemed to climb back into place.

Barry pressed me to go on; he felt he could get back to the hut in easy stages without assistance. I wanted to go on; but I also wanted to see him safely back to the hut. However, once he had demonstrated that he could operate alone, I opted to make for the top. It wasn't long before I was wishing I had returned to the river with Barry.

On one occasion a slipping boot left me hanging over a hundred feet of alpine air, and if the rock to which I clung with such desperation had shifted, that would have been my last dance on air. It became increasingly obvious why no one had attempted a frontal assault on the rock face . . . it was a challenge to fools or experts. Yet at around 4,500ft (1350 metres) the terrain levelled off and it was possible finally to walk upright. Truly, that was a glorious feeling.

And I thought about it as four chamois whistled at my unexpected intrusion before bounding off for a few yards and continuing their leisurely feeding. It was just such a feeling which made the whole life in the West Coast bush such a marvellous experience. And these experiences came so often, sometimes a fleeting delight; sometimes a lasting pleasure. It might be a view; it was often the sense of Nature's majesty. Certainly, it affected me more the longer I remained on the Coast, and the fact that I began shooting animals with film instead of bullets was a part of it. But more of that anon.

The task of making the top of Mt Datamos was relatively easy once the rock faces had been conquered, and by midday I was on the very summit nibbling at a bar of chocolate. I could see clear down the Arawata and Waitoto rivers in one direction, while the dark waters of Lake Leeb nestling above the Saxifrage Ridge looked like painted steel. It was possible through the camera's telephoto lens to detect a jetboat foaming up the Arawata.

The contrast between the slopes leading off the Haast Range into the Arawata and into the Waitoto were so different that it was like looking into two entirely different sections of alpine country. It made me think. But there was really little enough time for that because I had to get down the way I had come up. In the tussock slopes I passed ten chamois lying in the sun. When I caught sight of them I thought I'd climb down quietly with camera at the ready and record their siesta, but a kea gave warning of my approach, and he found his nosy way into my film record instead of the chamois. The return was easier, despite a few false attempts at finding "easy" ridges, and my day was made when I found Barry in such reasonable shape when I got back. His tale of woe included putting his feet through the bottom of the canoe, sinking it in the river and losing his camera.

We had one more major expedition, to Moonraker, during this trip, and it brought home the lesson all hunters must remember: don't ever overdo the mountain work, or the risk factor will rise dramatically. The mountains will be there next year or in ten years. We'd already had one warning with Barry's nasty fall on Mt Datamos, and were fortunate that it had not turned out more seriously than cuts and bruises.

A heavy frost decorated the ground and the boulders along the river edge. In places there were patches of ice. And through the still morning air came the roar from a stag echoing around the high granite bluffs. Barry led the way through a thick matting of vines as we headed for a likely ridge to lead us on to the open tops clinging to the steep sides of Mt Moonraker. We climbed steadily for an hour before taking a spell.

In heavy bush to our left a stag began to challenge our intrusion in his domain. His deep-throated roar became almost a frenzy as we answered him. I began quietly to edge forward and saw the old fellow lashing the bracken with his antlers.

Hoping to get closer I crawled to a large clump of fern and got the shock of my life when a hind burst from its centre with her feet threshing. She had obviously been resting in the fern when I actually stepped over her. We climbed higher and found a hind and a yearling feeding, while a large buck chamois lay in the open enjoying the sunshine. And then we began to zigzag our way towards the towering peak of Moonraker, arriving amongst the scattered areas of loose snow by midday.

To the south lay the head of the Waipara, and by gazing down to the west we could almost see the confluence where it joined with the mighty Arawata.

After a rest we turned north along the Haast Range and followed the top, where this was possible, to the 6200ft (1890 metres) Corner Post Peak. But we were finding the need to rest came more and more frequently. As the day wore on we wore out, and it became increasingly obvious we had overstepped the margin of our fitness. Places which we could, a few hours earlier, have scaled effortlessly became barriers which had to be circled, and the descent to the hut took much longer than we had planned. We had achieved a considerable amount of serious climbing during our month in the Waitoto region, but our performance on the Moonraker made it clear that we had done slightly more than our bodies were prepared to stand. If we had carried on, the risks of accident would have increased.

The next time we went up the Waitoto River we did it in style -- by jetboat. This eliminated the most uninteresting eight miles of the journey up, and let us out at the first gorge. Barry led and set a blistering pace towards Casey's Flats, and within half an hour we had almost walked into a hind and yearling as they dashed through the open bush before a stag came bounding out from behind a large windfall. I managed to get a fairly clear shot, and the headskin made up for the poorness of the antlers.

So we had achieved a success by the time we arrived at the rusty, galvanised shelter known as Casey's Hut, a trip accomplished well ahead of our programme because of the lift from the meat-hunter's jetboat. Barry and I decided to stock the larder as deer sign was obvious, and while he went downstream I tried the region behind the hut. A game trail gave me a quick access to an area about 600 feet above

Looking into the Waipara River, south of the Corner Post Peak on the Haast Range.

the Flats, and I soon had a couple of hinds lined up as I poked the rifle through a tree fork and waited. With the cross-hairs lined on the animal's neck I squeezed on the trigger, and we had venison.

Unfortunately I missed a stag on the way back. but managed another hind on the river's edge not far from the hut itself. Barry had no luck, but tea was ready as I fleshed my headskins.

On the following day he and I began a climb up an almost vertical rock slide towards the southern end of Cairn Ridge, and we managed to make the top after an occasional precarious piece of climbing by around 10.30am. Ahead on a rocky outcrop stood four chamois, but they offered us no interest. At around 4500 feet (1370 metres) the open tops were extremely weatherbeaten, and great terraces of rock shelved down to the bushline above the Te Naihi River. We could see into the head of the Murray River and, after reaching the jagged peak of the "Wart", we could see the watershed of the Turnbull and the Te Naihi.

Chamois made their appearance regularly, though in small numbers, and Barry managed to make some long shots pay off, but it wasn't until we had descended to the area opposite the impressive Lake Selbourne that deer were seen. We were heading down out of the lake towards Casey's Flats, where there was a drop off to an almost vertical cliff, the fall being about 400ft to 500ft, with a series of waterfalls down the side. We made our way down through a section of bush until halted by a rock wall with a drop of perhaps 100 feet to another patch of scrub. There was a crossing of about 50 feet with a greenish slime area in the centre of it, and seeping water. To avoid the crossing would have meant climbing back to the top of the basin and circling to the centre section of Casey's Creek.

We decided to give it a go because in the centre area there were a couple of rock ledges offering some assistance. I got across on to the first ledge, balanced rather

Taken from below Knobs Point, looking to the lake in the head of the Waitoto Valley.

like a man walking a wire, and then lunged on to the second. Success depended on maintaining momentum and balance. There were twelve to fifteen feet to go, so without breaking step I carried on towards the far side. About halfway across I began to slip on the moss and had a momentary feeling of panic that the old number might have come up, but my momentum kept me going, and a handy piece of supplejack enabled me to swing myself around into the bush.

Barry had watched my suicidal act and showed a lot more judgement than I had done in opting not to try it but to go up through the bush, even though it involved a big climb and walk. I was somewhat shaken up by my experience on the rock and took rather less interest in game on the rest of the way down than perhaps I might have done, but there was no noise of shooting from Barry's direction so perhaps we had scared the animals away. The light was failing by the time I got to the edge of a fresh bush slip and spotted deer on the far side. I dropped behind a fallen log, lined up an animal and brought it down. With time now at a premium, I skinned the head out to the base of the skull and cut straight down the back to between the shoulders, stuffed the back steaks down my shirt, the headskin over my shoulder, and dashed off into the dusk.

Darkness fell as I reached the base of the mountain, and I was forced to use a creek as my means of progress, sometimes having to wade with the water chest-high. This brought me out to the edge of the Waitoto and I headed along to where Barry had set out a candle as a beacon.

Despite all my derring-do on the rock face. Barry had beaten me back to the hut without taking stupid risks, so we devised "Harker's Rule", that the shortest route between two points is not always a straight line!

CHAPTER SIX

LUCK CAN BE A LADY

LOOKING BACK on years spent in the West Coast bush and on its precipitous mountains, and relating to my numerous expeditions with companions or alone the total of serious accidents which befell us, I can only feel that Fortune smiled benignly upon us. In the earlier years we took risks, often in ignorance but occasionally in high spirits, but as I grew older in the lore of the bush and the high country we took fewer and fewer chances. It would be useless to deny an occasional stupidity, like going hunting in carpet slippers, but the longer I spent in the mountains the greater was my respect for Nature's power both of creation and for destruction.

Sometimes, of course, there were situations created by others over which I had no control, especially in the air when using helicopters or fixed-wing aircraft. These one had simply to accept; to hope or pray when they occurred; to avoid the possibilities as far as possible of putting myself in the same position again. I recall two such incidents in a single day. We were flying in a fixed-wing plane, over the clearing in which a sawmill was operating, and the pilot was chatting to me over his shoulder as he watched the operation below us. When I looked up and saw a bush-covered ridge immediately ahead my heart filled my mouth to an extent that I was speechless. I thumped the pilot and pointed; he pulled sharply on the controls with a good flier's instinct for survival — but it was so close that we took the top off the trees on the ridge, and these were still caught up in the undercarriage when we landed.

But if that was not enough, we were in trouble a bare ten minutes later while flying up a very tight valley which, the pilot explained, would enable us to nip over the rim at the far end and save flying time. However, the further we flew in, the "heavier" the plane seemed to get. It wasn't lifting, and the pilot decided that survival rested on a very tight turn.

"Hang on, mate, we're going round," he shouted. I don't know how he managed it because my eyes were glued shut in fear, but in pub talk later I averred that the fixed undercarriage was actually rubbing the rock face of the valley as he made the turn. The years have convinced me of it. Anyway, I gave up flying for a while after that to allow the odds to settle down.

It is necessary to emphasise here that these accounts of accidents and near-accidents — of hits and misses — occurred over several years in some of the

Bannoch Brae Range, showing the Maitahi (*bottom left*) as a mere ditch in comparison. In such rugged country the risk of accidents was greatly increased.

roughest country in New Zealand. I do not want to give the impression that the world began to shake every time we set foot in the bush or on a mountain. These episodes have been culled from experiences during six years of hunting and climbing . . . six years spent in a dangerous occupation made more so by the distance separating people in the bush from normal facilities. It is something which the weekend shooter or holiday tramper must keep always to the forefront of his mind: when he is in the bush on the West Coast he is a long way from help of any description. To an extent, at least, the greatly increased population of airborne Coasters has balanced the odds to a degree; the helicopters have been a really magnificent rescue vehicle.

Mt Allen, 1968. Barry McClausland and I were out after game and we had climbed only a short distance from the valley floor when we split company. I climbed on to near where some high rocky outcrops began, and on top of one of these stood a chamois, a quite easy shot from my position, so I bopped it. Unfortunately, it fell down a sheer face and lodged on a ledge about halfway to the floor beneath, a most frustrating situation. I moved around to get a good sight of the face and reckoned that I could just about reach it with some sharp mountain climbing and push the animal off the ledge with a drop then of about fifty feet.

I nuzzled my way along the rock face, clutching at every handhold, shuffling my feet carefully along the narrow ledge, unable to move any way but sideways. When I reached the point immediately above where the chamois lay, the inability to manoeuvre became a definite drawback. He was lodged just a couple of feet below me, yet I was unable to tickle him off the ledge with my toe. I took a firmer hold on the rock outcrop supporting me and tried to use both feet to kick him off. That was disaster point: my handhold dislodged under the additional strain and I executed a back-flip which on later reflection, I considered would have looked rather well at a swimming pool. When I came back to consciousness I was lying alongside the chamois, and waking brought the pain. It gave me some idea of what it felt like to be run over by a steamroller. I thought my troubles were mainly abrasions and bruises, so forced myself to skin the chamois and take the head; I didn't feel up to carrying the carcase because of a pain in my chest. When I got off Mt Allen the pain in my chest turned out to be two fractured ribs.

On another occasion, again when hunting chamois in the Bettison Stream area, I had shot three animals and was in the process of gutting them. The first two were cleaned and ready for pickup, but the third must only have been stunned, for as I rolled it on to its back it kicked out viciously and one of its horns caught inside my bush shirt. As the animal struggled the horn opened up a wound with the precision of a scalpel down several inches of my arm.

As I said earlier, there were times when I foolishly invited trouble, and one of the worst of these occurred in the headwaters of the Waitaha while hunting with Barry Petrie and Paul Bevernage. We were moving up Reid Creek and found our passage blocked by a narrow, steeply formed glacier. To detour would have cost time (and we had plenty of that), so with a "one-two-three-and-away" I stupidly tried to run across it at a 45-degree angle. The immediate impetus of my dash took me practically halfway across before I became airborne. I thumped heavily on to the ice and began sliding down it like a log on skid row. I remember at some stage my rifle passing several feet above my head, as I slid right down the glacier and fell off the end of it. Unfortunately for my comfort, I landed on my tailbone and this left me semi-crippled for a while, and limited my activity to creeping around the camp. Indeed, as one of my hunting mates pointed out at the time, I looked like Wyatt Earp in the "draw" position for several days as I repented my foolishness.

Once when I was hunting with Teddy Meadows we had slogged our way into the head of the Balfour, a tributary of the Cook, and our passage took us around the bottom of a cliff on top of which was a large icefield. We passed around the base, and carried on some four or five hundred yards when there was a sharp report like the crack of a rifle. We turned to see a huge formation of ice peel off the cliff and smash itself to pieces on the path we had so recently vacated. Luck was certainly a lady that day, and Teddy and I spent a lot of time during the next few hours discussing what might have occurred if we had done this, that, or some other thing to delay our tramp around the base of that cliff by five or ten minutes . . .

Stories of lucky escapes while working the helicopters are legion. There are a lot of other stories which are not told because the participants do not survive to tell them. The difference so often is a matter of luck. Once I was sitting on a helicopter skid as the pilot brought the machine in close to recover shot game, ready to jump when the distance was right. Something he saw, but which I did not, caused him to give the machine power and lift it away just as I dropped off. The apex of my fall was about 20 feet from the ground, but I was doubly fortunate that it was not higher, and that I landed in swampy ground which cut the risk of breaking my legs off at the knees.

A normal load for a Hiller 12E. Five deer and six chamois being lifted from our camp following two days' footshooting. At times, considerable risks were taken to collect carcases from cliff ledges or tight rocky canyons.

The late Tony Hawker was a top helicopter pilot, but lost his life in a flying accident at Haast.

Attaching chains for a heavy lift. An engine failure at this point would obviously pose problems for the man on the ground.

The work from helicopters is so difficult that I am surprised there are not more accidents than already occur. Men have been beheaded, caught by the tail rotor, dropped from great heights by broken strops or operational error, fallen over bluffs while recovering shot game . . . the list is endless and tragic. Yet some go on for years while some last only months or weeks.

I once invited an enthusiastic but inexperienced youngster to join me hunting Angora goat in the Porerua Valley. Just a day trip, nothing strenuous or too exciting. When we got to a very wide part of the stream I told him to cross and hunt the other side, but on no account to shoot across the river towards me. Thus, we would be moving up each side of the river, so safety demanded no cross shooting. The warning seemed so obvious that I did not labour the point.

I was some five or six yards in from the river which, while out of sight was still within hearing in the bush, when my young companion began peppering my area like Errol Flynn winning the war in the Pacific. Bullets whipped around my ears like wasps, and I clawed at the ground shouting abuse while awaiting the emptying of his magazine (he was using a .303 with a ten-shot mag.) and the opportunity to put my point of view rather more forcibly face-to-face. My language that day would not have been suitable for the vicar's soiree, I can tell you, though I calmed down later and tried to give my advice to him in a more acceptable manner. Apparently he had seen four or five goats browsing across the river, and though I had been unable to see them through the bush, they had been quite close to me. His enthusiasm for the hunt had proved too strong, and the chance for a skin had simply wiped out all memory of the careful warnings I had given him.

Rock falls and avalanches scared the daylights out of me, especially after one of them crippled my father during a hunting stroll with his rifle. Luck was hardly with him then, as it was with me when I was climbing in the Gunn Creek area near the Perth River. I was moving slowly up a section both steep and narrow having just clambered over the side of a waterfall. It narrowed even further as I moved up and, while stopping to rest I heard all sorts of banging and crashing from above. The sounds were the clue. As quickly as I was able in the conditions I scrambled to a large overhanging rock and crawled as far under it as I could do.

Time is hard to estimate in such circumstances, but it was about forty seconds later that a couple of large boulders came tearing through the bush and landed in the creek. These were followed by a hail of smaller stones, including some about the size of a rugby ball and a few the size of a tea chest. The deluge went on for the best part of a minute, though it seemed considerably longer as I crouched under my protective rock. The air was alive with dust and dirt, the remains of a huge rock-slide which had begun some distance above and crashed its way down to the creek where I had been standing. A few minutes earlier - or later - would have almost certainly resulted in my being caught by the slide. The defile from which I had just climbed when the first rocks arrived was filled to a depth of ten or twelve

An ice ridge over the head of Chainmans Creek in the Mt Hitchen area. Where there was ice deteriorating in the summer months, there was also danger from avalanches and slips.

feet with rubble and boulders, so it was an understatement to suggest I was shaken by the experience.

I spent a lot of time during the rest of that day stopping for a listen and a look, and reconsidering the rock-slide. It is the kind of thing which does happen at the end of the winter months, often because ice has formed between boulders and forced them out, so that when the ice melts the rocks tend to be unstable. Sometimes it occurs the other way: melting ice forms rivulets which undermine the rocks and set them moving. Whatever the reason, the safest means of combating the problem is to be somewhere else when the rock-slide occurs or to get there as quickly as possible, as I was fortunate enough to be able to do in Gunn Creek that day.

My father had no such luck. His misfortune occurred back in 1964 down near a construction camp at Haast when the tourist road was still being built. He and mum were enjoying a caravan tour, but my father was a very keen and accomplished hunter, and he filled his days shooting for venison and velvet when the weather was suitable. He used to drive out to an area, park the car and follow the bulldozer tracks to find suitable game areas reasonably easy of access.

One deer feeding ground was reached from the shores of Lake Moeraki after an

On the slopes of Miserable Ridge in the Mikonui catchment area, showing the type of broken terrain from which helicopters had to retrieve the animals we shot on foot.

Taken with a standard lens from the shooting position on a helicopter. The rotor blades are almost touching the snow tussock.

uphill climb of some 200 yards to a fringe of heavy timber. The area was blessed with good feed, and deer appeared about the same time each day. My father studied the behaviour pattern of the animals for a couple of days before deciding on a stalk which would take him to the clearing edge slightly before the deer.

On the day of the hunt he gathered his gear, and mum decided she would go along as well, remaining in the car with her book to while away a pleasant afternoon. Her decision to go was rather the exception than the rule, but it was to prove very advantageous and, indeed, a lifesaving one that particular day. The car was parked at the lake edge and my father began his climb to the hide he had selected. He settled in comfortably to wait, the rifle against a log with the magazine clipped in place.

For ten minutes or so nothing much stirred. Then there was a clatter of stones from well above, suggesting that the expected animals were on the move. But the noise of the stones went on increasing and, to my father's horror, the trees and ground began to sway and tremble. Then there was the sound of rock parting under tremendous stress. Father dropped his rifle and endeavoured to sprint away from the crumbling hillside, but he was not quick enough. A bouncing boulder grazed the side of his head and brought him first to his knees and then, apparently to unconsciousness. As he lay he was engulfed by a moving mountainside of rubble — a huge slip which swept everything from its path or rolled inexorably over it.

Back at the lakeside the thunderous roar reached my Mother still sitting in the car. She looked up to see a virtual wall of rock and trees tumbling towards the lake. The whole gigantic mess swept past the car about twenty-five yards away and cascaded into the lake, converting the placid waters into the sort of bubbling pool one associates with Rotorua. For mum the scene had an additional dimension, for she quickly realised that Dad must have been caught up in it.

She was unable to turn the large car around on the narrow trail, so she did the next most sensible thing and set off on foot to get help from the Ministry of Works camp. A South Westland contractor, Maurie Roberts, quickly organised a rescue party and sent a convoy of earth-moving equipment roaring back to the site of the landslide. There were still small falls occurring, and the men seemed agreed that no one could have survived, so a message was sent back for transmission to the police at Whataroa. However, the telephone line was down and the road access out of Haast had been lost, but the radio telephone call was received by a fishing boat off the coast, and relayed to the police.

Meanwhile, deep in the slip my father had miraculously escaped death. Occasionally he would have brief periods of consciousness and then lapse back into blackness. A rock which had withstood the force of the slide, and a tree trunk which had acted as a wedge against the stones, had saved his life. His body had been twisted grotesquely about like a child's rag doll, yet he was able to see above him a circle of daylight, as boulders still danced overhead. His muffled shouts drew the attention of a group of rescuers, who took considerable risks when dashing across the still-moving rubble to pinpoint my father's whereabouts.

Once they found him the obvious need was for medical assistance, but recent floods had put the road out and closed the airfield. To the men who found him battered, broken and bleeding, physical obstacles were put before them merely to be overcome. They set to work and cleared the damaged airstrip so that a Dominie aircraft could get in. It was thanks to their efforts that my father was able to get crucial medical attention so rapidly — a doctor accompanied him on the flight to Hokitika — and that he was not only able eventually to get about, but still go hunting and fishing.

Although the accident might have inhibited his ability to tramp and climb, it certainly didn't affect his eyesight! I remember an occasion in 1970 when the late Frank Smith — he was killed in Canada — offered us a lift in his jetboat up the Paringa river to a spot which left us a three-mile walk to the hut across riverflat and bush track. We took it easy, and made our first break on the river's edge, where a chain of bluffs forced a shallow crossing. Dad pointed out a deer which he could see feeding on a grassy slip.

Now I was no slouch on the eyesight, but I couldn't see that deer. Dad explained exactly where it was, and the direction it faced. Despite the fact I thought he was pulling the "young fella's" leg, I took out the binoculars and focused on the slip. Sure enough, a hind was feeding in the open.

I remembered this trip in for another, less edifying reason. A few months earlier I had carried in 50 yards of aerial and transmitter wire, and some mean hound had pinched the lot. What possible use it could have had to anyone I simply couldn't understand, but it was an unfortunate fact of life in the mountains that there was always one bad apple around who would steal the eye from a needle.

The author's father and Stuart Menzies at the Top Hut in the Karangarua Valley, years after Ken Harker's crippling accident near Lake Moeraki in 1964. He was determined to continue to enjoy shooting — and he did so!

But worse was to come. Dad and I had first intended to fly into the area by light plane, but had been unable to arrange the flight for the day we wanted, and had been happy to accept Frank Smith's jetboat offer. Just as well! Dad told me when I brought in a hind the next morning that the landing strip had two deep holes deliberately dug across it. If we had come in by plane, the likelihood was that we would have all have landed up in the river with the aircraft. Why people develop such kinks I can never understand.

Dad was always eager to get into the mountains, and he was along at the beginning of 1971 when we organised an expedition for Stuart Menzies, camera-totin' expert from the *Christchurch Star*, operating from the cabin at the head of the Karangarua River. On that occasion I think I got nine deer and six chamois in three days -- and Stuart got some magnificent game and mountain shots. Indeed, my father tended to act as a good omen on my trips with him, for the last time we were out on an organised expedition in 1972 I had a pretty good return on venison. Few of those who helped drag him from the rock slide in 1964 would ever have expected him to be able to go back into the mountains, but he did. And he will again.

One accident which really caused a great deal of concern and could have had fatal consequences involved Paul Bevernage when we were hunting well up the Mikonui above the Dickson confluence. Paul spotted a young stag, and though it

Winter or summer there is constant danger in country like this — above the Whataroa.

was an awkward shot in the fading light he managed to drop it in its tracks. But it was not dead, so we dashed up to deliver the coup-de-grace. I held its ears while Paul held its jaw with one hand, and went to use his knife with the other. The stag flexed himself and gave a final kick so that Paul missed with his knife and slashed the blade across his wrist. Blood spurted in every direction, and it was soon obvious we had a serious accident on our hands which no amount of sticking-plaster or torn strips of handkerchief were going to fix. Paul tried to staunch the flow of blood with a bush singlet as he set off down the river to where we had left the car, some two miles away.

   I quickly gutted the stag, tossed it on to my back. grabbed the rifles and set off after Paul. His trail of blood was easy to follow. There was a record regulation-breaking drive to hospital, where Paul was by now too weak to walk inside, but the Hokitika surgical team soon worked him over. He had lost a lot of blood and it was the type of accident which can happen so easily to hunters. There is a minimum of precaution which can be taken, except care when handling the knife.

CHAPTER SEVEN

MEMORIES ARE MADE . . . .

SOME TRIPS spring to memory because of the shooting successes, or perhaps a particularly good trophy or an unusually funny occurrence, but I recall a 1967 trip into the headwaters of the Adams River because it was one of the most trying I experienced on the Coast. Even retrospect has not dulled the sharper edges of memory to make this one anything but a nightmare. "Flick" Harrop, from Upper Hutt, was my companion, and freezing-cold weather the cross we had eventually to bear.

The Adams River begins a turbulent life from the Adams icefall, and its headwaters are hemmed by the Adams Col, Angel Col and Guardian Peak, while the lower barrier is formed by Speculation Hill, Mt Lambert and Mt Kensington. Just to make matters really difficult for the tramper and hunter, the river runs into a series of tight, impassable gorges, the worst of which is called the Eblis after an evil spirit.

But Flick and I were not concerned when we started in good weather. I had been into the region before and I knew the Adams could provide exciting shooting, even though the riverflats nestled under the Arethusa Icefall and the dominant Guardian Peak could prove a trap for the unwary. We were well laden, eager to give the region a fair amount of our time, as we waded through the crystal clear Wanganui River and made our way under a brilliant blue sky across the mouth of the Hot Springs Creek towards Speculation Spur. We managed a steady pace to the old culler's track where a rest period ended prematurely when we gave best to the sandflies and started to work our way up the gradual spur.

It was here that Flick managed a snap shot at a largish stag as it took off down into the tall timber. He had reason to be pleased with this early success for the animal had a fine rack of eleven tines, each almost jet black in colour with brilliant white tips. We removed the head and hung it above the track for collection on our return.

We trudged on and did not manage a sighting again until we finally broke through the alpine scrub to step on to the open snow grass tops. Our line took us steadily to the top of Speculation Spur where we were able to rest and gaze into the impressive hanging basin that is the watershed of Hot Springs Creek. The sides of Speculation fall away quite rapidly, so game trails are etched deeply into the contours and, as we watched, six chamois in single file ambled towards the safety of Boulderpool Stream where they were joined by two others.

Flick Harrop crossing the Adams, a mere 500 or so yards from the terminal face of the glacier, just below our campsite.

The weather was still fine and our spirits were high as we followed the same game trail, sometimes on our backsides because of its steepness, and in just over an hour we were more than two thirds of the way off the valley floor. We sheltered from the intense heat of the sun in the shade of an overhanging boulder while we put up a haze of cigarette smoke and looked over the open moraine flats. Almost immediately we saw two large stags and perhaps a dozen hinds lying in the shade in portions of the river where it made a lazy S-turn after breaking free from the icepack.

Further up the flats, where rock bluffs hold back the total collapse of the snow tussock and mountain scrub, we could make out the small shapes of chamois as they too lay in shaded areas. Flick was excited at the number of game so readily visible. We worked it out that the deer would likely move up the valley and climb a short distance to the right-hand side of the valley where there were rocky crags and boulders offering hiding places from human intruders. So without thought of concealment we moved down into the valley proper, and finally stood on the edge of the Adams.

It was bliss to shed those heavy packs and douse our faces in the cold water, letting it trickle down our backs. Once we had cooled off, we sorted out a satisfactory campsite of fern shelter and firewood. We built a generous fireplace, collected armsful of grass for bedding, and the tent went up in a setting of quite superb beauty. It seemed a blasphemy to have instant spuds and saveloys in such a beautiful spot. It was definitely chicken-and caviare-territory.

But Flick had no time for such thoughts. His mind and eye were filled with game and he was determined to use the couple of hours before nightfall to go after the stags. I settled for a stroll, following the Adams along the west bank and noticing in the discoloured waters a swirl which suggested caution would be needed in a crossing. Flick would have had less trouble in fording further up near the terminal ice face.

I had strolled to my limit and was about to turn back when I spotted a fine

10-pointer feeding on the far side of the river. With time aplenty I took careful aim and missed. Needless to say, there was no second opportunity.

Back at camp Flick had hot cocoa ready and a spindly 12-pointer head. Its bad point was the lack of thickness in the timber, something which in my experience was most unusual in the Wanganui River region deer herds. But poor old Flick had paid some penalty: in his excitement to get back to camp he had forgotten the camera around his neck when making a river crossing. When he went down, the camera went under and suffered a good ducking.

That evening things really started to go awry. The sky clouded over and the temperature plunged. Around midnight the rains came, and with each hour they seemed to be lashed into greater fury, drenching the region with a torrent of water. It was so heavy that our best efforts couldn't keep the rain from getting into our tent, and we were already shivering when the sleet began. The tent walls billowed in and out like a clown's cheeks as the wind slashed straight off the icefall.

Flick was unused to such conditions, and gave me his views of hunting in straight terms: "To hell with you, Harker. A joker must be off his wick to enjoy this type of hunting."

However, he cheered up visibly when I assured him that he could have come into the region when the weather was *really* bad! We didn't get much sleep that night, and the next day brought rain . . . more rain . . . and even more rain. The transistor radio, between static and fadeout, offered little hope, and with the sky promising snow I decided that our best decision was the only one: pack up and get out in a hurry.

Flick was no more eager than I to spend another night frozen and wet, and I was particularly keen to avoid having to tackle the heavy bush flanking the Eblis Gorge once there was a heavy coating of snow on the steep side of Speculation Spur. So a quick hot meal of soup cooked over solid fuel blocks gave us the impetus to pack our wet gear and begin a two hour-and-a-half climb up the sides of the now swollen Boulderpool Creek. Rain continued to lash us and we were soon drenched despite oilskin clothing, and as well as my personal discomfort I had an additional concern that the mist shrouding the tops might conceal our way off them.

Our earlier litterbug performance in casting orange peel from us during a rest period when we had viewed the Hot Springs basin turned out to be a morale booster in showing that we were where we should have been. We had to proceed with considerable caution through the swirling mist, for there was a visibility of only about thirty feet, but my yodel echoed through the valley when the first of my red plastic tape signs appeared, tied on to the alpine scrub. The success must have gone to my head, for I immediately made a stupid mistake.

We should leave the ridge, I suggested, and cut down into the Wanganui riverbed at a point which I predicted would be opposite the confluence of Hendes Creek. On a clear day it would have been quite plain that we were still too far up the ridge to enable a descent to be effectively made, but on this day there was a virtual whiteout

That dot between the chamois' eyes is a bullet hole — more from luck than by design. While meat-hunting in Architects Creek the author was carrying a deer back to camp and almost fell over the chamois, which was feeding under an overhanging ledge. The chamois was shot from the hip.

A chamois on the skyline of Headlong Spur.

The broken mountainsides overlooking Hot Springs Creek in the Wanganui River area would, by all accounts, be the toughest terrain for mountain travel in the South Westland ranges.

with heavy rain to boot. There were places where we had to hang on largely with willpower, and poor old Flick became tangled in almost every vine, giving me a tongue-lashing with each mishap to relieve his frustration.

It was really tough going, and as one who spent most of my time in the mountains I had some idea of how poor Flick, without this advantage, must be feeling. We finally broke through the bush and found ourselves on a shingle beach between two bluffs — and the Wanganui a raging torrent of floodwater, affording no chance for a crossing. Huddled miserably together under a dripping, moss-covered rock overhang we smoked disconsolately through cupped hands in an effort to keep the fags dry enough to draw, and stared at the foaming river as it roared past us carrying branches and debris.

Coming down through the bush in torrential rain had been a daunting enough task, but we'd had at least the advantage then of thinking we were making our way towards the way out and better times. Now however, we knew we had to climb the almost vertical sides to bypass the seeming never-ending series of bluffs, and our spirits were very, very low. But we kept at it, hour after bloody hour, until we stumbled on to Hot Springs Flat with the torrential rain now running down our necks and out the legs of our shorts. Even as I recall the circumstances now I can conjure up again just how really miserable I felt.

There was no chance of fording the river to reach the car, parked about 500 yards away downstream on the north bank so we had to continue down river through the bush and across the remaining flats. Wilberg Creek was a tough barrier which we had to overcome, with waist-high water all but sweeping us off our weary feet, and then there was a longish walk of a mile or so out to the road. By the time we got to Hendes Ferry Flick was stumbling, so I left him in the warm company of some students occupying the old converted farm building and slow-jogged round to the Wanganui River quarry to collect the car.

My own shoulders ached for days after that trip, and I later got a letter from Flick stating that he had extended his vacation by a week after coming out of the Adams River — simply sitting in his local hotel, moving only when he had to.

Some sections of the South Westland ranges can be difficult enough without the additional problems of a quick change in the weather or a quick rise in the river levels, and it's as well to know the worst pieces of tiger country before venturing too far into "the interior". One of the areas which has a place near the top of my toughest-trip list is that in from the Waitaha River in the Mt Barry region and beyond. John Hardy, Robbie Scott, Joe Whitman and I had decided to go after chamois on Mt Neville during the middle of 1969 and that trip showed the need for hunters to be in peak physical condition to attempt the area.

Indeed, looking back through some of my old maps recently I noticed the number of markings of "thick bush" and "rough" which I had put in during the years I was moving regularly through these areas.

But my mates and I were in great trim, and once we crested Headlong Spur and

In the Lower Waitaha Valley above the Douglas Creek confluence, where a rope provided the only way up and over the bluff.

A young stag, his ears up at the click of the camera, feeding on the edge of Moonbeam Torrent Slip.

moved on towards Mt Neville, the next mountain seemed to offer even better opportunities. All that was involved was extra distance, so it was on with the motley. This was a mistake. It was not planned, and so we had not kept to a high level route which would have drastically reduced our travelling time. However, it all seems so much easier in hindsight, or on the second time around. So we kept just above the alpine scrubline and maintained a gutbusting pace to kill the additional distance -- until confronted with a series of steep bluffs to the nor-east.

These troublesome pieces of country caused us no end of bother. The first of the bluffs proved awkward to bypass because the lower end dropped off sheer for at least 350 feet, while the top portion rose steeply to meet another perpendicular bluff supporting a semicircular platform. Using the rope I managed to secure sufficient handholds to worm my way slowly to the top, and then began the tedious task of hauling packs and people up. We had quite a lot of this sort of work because the type of bluff we struck there seemed to have been repeated over and over again in Nature's design.

One of them almost cost a life. We had reached a steepish drop of perhaps sixty feet or so and, finding there was simply no way of climbing around it in the usual practice we had adopted, we decided to rope over the side and follow a narrow ledge for some twelve yards until the rock angled off at a slight slant which would allow a route down. Robbie went first, followed by Joe. I was next man on that totem pole and John was to swing down on a looped rope.

When I reached the comparative safety of the ledge, I swung my pack across my knees and started slowly working down the steep, smooth rock face, using my backside as a brake. Halfway down I froze to the rock with the sound of a scream from above. John came hurtling down through the air, a confusion of arms and legs, having missed the ledge by inches on his swing. He crashed heavily on to the top edge of the slanted rock and disappeared from view. There was a total silence . . . the sort of silence which often accompanies fear. A loud silence.

Everyone began activating the situation at once. I threw my pack down the last few yards, while willing hands reached for my rifle and camera to allow me easier access to the ledge above me. Gazing over the top I was able to give an elated whoop, mixed with surprise I must admit, for barely three yards from the side, caught up in supplejack and bush-lawyer lay John, dazed but apparently otherwise unharmed. Indeed, as he began to sense the fortune of his escape he soon got himself organised and offered a few well-chosen words of praise for the supplejack, the sort of compliments usually reserved for orchids. It had played a key role in saving him from disappearing off the rocks into space and, perhaps, to a landing which offered death. But in the way of the mountains and hunting, not too much time is wasted on what-might-have-been. That is left for the bar-room and later embroidery. So it was onward and downward to safer ground.

Later, as the long fingers of red and gold played across the sky from a sinking sun, we came upon one of the best camp sites it was ever my pleasure to discover . . . well . . . stumble into. On the open top of a spur which offered a commanding view of the Waitaha River and the Moonbeam Torrent there was an area of ground so weather-worn that large rocks thrust weirdly out from the snowgrass. One of these was carved by the erosive force of wind and rain on an angle so that the top edge overhung a neighbouring stone column.

This afforded us a completely rain and wind-proof shelter which was made attractive and even more useful by a large tarn a mere stone's throw away.

We cut armfuls of snow tussock to cover the floor area and then spread the tent over it before slumping down ourselves. Billies strung over the fire, cigarettes drawing well and music from Joe's mouth organ drifting around us, it was relaxing to lie there and watch the last of the sunlight slide off the Hitchen Range. If ever there was a need to justify tramping or climbing or hunting or anything else to do with the mountains, we found it that day. The mountains and valleys of South Westland have left me with thousands of marvellous memories, but few drift so perfectly through my mind as that corner of paradise on a June day in 1969.

Hunting was the name of the game, and up to that time the animals we had seen had been of a routine nature, with a marked absence of deer. Robbie and Joe had both secured rather worthwhile chamois heads, and as John was the sole North Island member of the party it was decided that he should get a decent set of horns and, until he did, the first shot at sightings would be at his discretion.

The campsite was so delightful that we decided to use it as a base rather than climb further, so our shooting plans were for the immediate vicinity. We climbed

The Lower Otoko Pass, between the head of the Clarke and the head of the Otoko, was extremely tough travelling for the footshooter, but this was made up for by the excellent chamois hunting that the area afforded.

Another view of the Otoko Pass, where rock and ice falls were commonplace.

The rough tangle of vegetation in Hawkins Creek during a spell of wet weather — and an inquiring look from a chamois forced out into the open from his shelter beneath the rocks.

as a group, making our way steadily upward until the snow and ice made it necessary to sidle. By this time at this height chamois were plentiful and John had little trouble in securing two beauties, making five trophy heads in two days.

We worked the Mt Barry area pretty extensively, exploring rather than shooting. and deciding that we were fortunate in our fitness. It was not country to which the inexperienced or the unfit should be encouraged to enter.

We were having an entertaining time on the mountainside when we felt the first large drops of rain. The sky was almost cloudless, so we assumed it was merely a sun-shower, but decided nevertheless to move down and towards our grand little camp on the spur to the left of Moonbeam Torrent, marked from well above by its adjacent tarn. Within an hour the sky had changed to a leaden grey with a darker cloudbank pushing across the north.

It looked like snow weather on the way, so we decided to pack the gear and hit the trail for home to avoid any possibility of being snowed in. This time we followed a high-level route above those cursed bluffs, and made the top edge of Headlong Spur in good time because we had maintained an almost crippling pace. We lost valuable time searching for my special tape marker, and in the end we decided to make camp nearby rather than risk a descent in the darkness down the Spur towards Bartrum Creek and then on to the hut overlooking Whirling Water.

Our tent was insufficient cover against the lashing of rain that night. Water seeped under our groundsheets until the ground inside became almost as wet as that outside, and then it simply flowed through, turning our sleeping bags into containers of messy feathers. There was no need to discuss the decision to quit camp at first light, and with rain still coming down in bucketfuls we moved as quickly as we could through the alpine scrub and down to the Bartrum Creek waterfalls. The water coming down the Bartrum was less than we expected, but Whirling Water certainly made up for it, and by the time we reached the Kiwi Flat hut we were all exhausted and hungry enough to eat possum.

We stoked up the fire, shed our soaking clothes and enjoyed the luxury of warmth and steaming hot, sweet tea as the rain continued unabated, and Whirling Water nearby lived up to its name.

To the uninitiated, finding four naked fellows shouting and laughing while their clothes steamed inside and the rain poured down outside might suggest an out-of-the-way extension to a mental hospital, but for those who climb and hunt it was really what it is all about: good company after time well spent on the mountains.

Barry Petrie, Pete Billington, Paul Bevernage and I did a lot of hunting together over the years, covering a mighty stretch of South Westland territory. The "Old Firm" had its successes and failures, but it always had spirit and an attitude which favoured having a go, whether it be the next peak, a trophy head roaming in the back of beyond, or a postprandial stroll with rifles or cameras along, just in case.

A few years ago all four of us set out and managed to climb to within 120 yards of the Clarke Pass at the head of the Paringa River before we were beaten back by

Drying out chamois headskins in the Valley of Darkness in 1969, when they were worth between $5 and $7 each. On one five-day expedition we brought out fifty-six, and got thirty-nine on a later, two-day expedition.

cold, sleet and a dangerously swirling fog. So near and yet so far. But with any but the "Old Firm" we would never have got so close in such horrible conditions. And so it was a very cold, miserable and depressed group who were forced to flee down the snow tussock to the old semi-collapsed Tunnel Creek hut for warmth and recuperation.

It was not until two years later that I managed to satisfy my ambition to conclude that journey, after climbing up McCullaugh Creek and following the mountainside around to the west. On that occasion — it was either late 1971 or early 1972 — my companion was a wellknown tramper, Terry Strutt, and one of the more notable aspects of the climb was the absence of game animals. We had sighted deer in the Creek, but after that in the open tops we saw only two chamois, and this proved particularly disappointing to Terry, who had an expensive camera and perfect weather — but few animal study opportunities.

We stood on the far side of the pass savouring the day and the view, and opted to try some scenic photography looking over "the roof of the South Island". There was a large upthrust of rock called Outpost which offered a challenge that Terry and I could not resist. Once we got on to it, however, the climb was easier than it had appeared from below and, except for a few shale slips of a minor nature, there was little to inhibit a fast trip up. The view was superb.

Outpost was aptly named, for it gave us a lofty perch with a view for miles in the diamond-hard brilliance of the summer day, clear as crystal and as beautiful to the eye. Terry had been climbing in the area the previous year with a North Island group on the Main Divide, and he pointed out the peaks they had climbed. Even from our distance those majestic tops are as memorable today as though I had taken colour movie film and was able to run it back through my mind. I guess that makes the occasion memorable?

In mid-1969 John Davis (Christchurch) and I were hunting the Hitchen area, seeking chamois on the southern spur bracing the slopes of MacGregor Creek, and the occasion is etched in my memory largely because it included a really dramatic stalk in circumstances of considerable danger.

I still twitch a bit when I think of that ridge, jagged and rocky, with flat portions of shale flaking off as we made each step along it. The sides pitched down the mountain at a hazardous angle, to say the least, and a long, long way below levelled into a narrow boulder-strewn creekbed which twisted through a canyon. I plastered myself against the rim and looked back at John, who was as ill at ease as I was. It was precarious terrain, and in the section in which we found ourselves it would have been possible to fall in three different directions with comparatively little chance of ever being able to tell the story of it. We could neither stand nor kneel with comfort, so had to continue moving crablike towards the safety of the last rocky outcrop. The thought of how we could possibly renegotiate the ridge back was causing me considerable concern.

I had indulged in some hair-raising stunts while out hunting, but the stalk along that dizzy ridge still gives me the jimjams.

We had spotted the chamois along a narrow ridge which runs in practically a straight line with Mt Smythe, and it seemed an easy stalk in our favour, with plenty of daylight to accomplish it. John and I decided that it could provide us with the conclusion to our hunt, but the chamois had different ideas. Perhaps we were too cocksure, but the animals moved gradually higher to the tip of the grass-capped ridge and disappeared. We followed in the general direction and the mountain began to get as steep as the roof of an old English church. But we were well embarked before we properly realised that the final few pelts were going to be a lot harder to obtain than we had considered.

Then the edge of the sheer drop came into view, and with the other side of our ridge being vertical, the only chance we had of following the mob was to keep on its tracks. The chamois were not too far ahead at this stage, with a large buck in the centre of half a dozen nannies which kept looking our way and giving the characteristic whistle.

So John and I sat and considered whether we should try and corner them, or retreat to the safety of the Hitchen slopes. At midday it was a choice with the odds weighted in favour of chasing the chamois, so on we went and soon realised that we had, in fact, got them virtually cornered. When we got into the tricky shale material we slithered along for fifteen yards or so, sweating. But the second section was so much worse that it made the first part seem like a paved footpath.

John was using a .333 OKH. (actually a necked-down .30-06) which he had used to shoot wild horses in the North Island, and he was breaking his neck (near enough to it in actuality at times) to get a crack at a large buck chamois. We had seen plenty of nannies during the day, and had let them be, but the buck ahead belonged to John. He reckoned it had his number on it.

Finally, we reached the safety of that last rocky outcrop, and as we set about getting a suitable shooting position my qualms about the return down the ridge disappeared in the excitement of the hunt.

John soon showed that the journey up the razorback ridge had not affected his hand or his eye, and he soon had the buck plus a couple of females sporting full winter pelts. Once he had bopped them we had to accomplish the trip back, and in spite of the higher octane rating of our blood after the excitement and reward of the stalk, the return was indescribable. However, once accomplished we were able to get down through the thick belt of alpine scrub to the dead chamois, it proved extremely worth while. The buck sported a fine set of 11 5/8in horns (295.28mm) with a beautiful headskin to match.

With the effort of fighting our way back up through the scrub, we were well and truly done in by the time we arrived at the snowgrass to stretch out and enjoy a cigarette. It was while lying on my stomach gazing across the neighbouring spurs that I caught a movement. I grabbed John's rifle and removed the 'scope caps to get a better view, and discovered it was a good-sized stag. And because it was on the terrain we would cross on our way home, that stag was legal tender.

A copybook stalk brought us to within a 100 yards or so of it and as John had no wish to shoot deer I removed my pack and rested the rifle over the shoulder strap to get a superb resting shot. The old fellow turned out to be a weak-antlered 12-pointer in good condition, so besides some juicy off-cuts there was a fine pelt to boot. And after such wonderful fortune it was pleasant to complete the walk out without mishap other than the collapse of my boots.

Whenever I recall that trip I think how much John Davis really deserved those fine horns and pelts after our experience on the slippery, shale ridge which had given us the advantage over the chamois.

CHAPTER EIGHT

UP THE CREEK

IN MID-1972 a keen Maniototo hunter from Wedderburn, George Lindsay, arrived on the Coast looking for sport and joined Bruce Wright and myself on a trip up the Maitahi River. In the way of things, the weather packed up almost as soon as we had got off the road and on to the rough tractor track which cut across the lower flats to the first river crossing. We abandoned my utility vehicle rather than risk having to dig it out of the bog, and set off up-river on foot, keeping to the south bank. This meant we had to wade only through a small portion of the river near the Longbluff Ford, which was lucky for us because the water levels were up and the likelihood of crossing the main river was remote.

As we squelched through the lower flats large mobs of cattle gazed at us with bovine cupidity — or so we thought as we gave them reasonable berth. But we soon realised that they were too waterlogged to do much running. The rain dropped to a fine drizzle, but we decided nevertheless to stay overnight at the first hut up-river, despite the fact it was only a few miles from our kickoff point.

It hardly seemed a good idea once we got inside and saw water puddled on the floor and seeping down the walls and in the corners. I had been through the region occasionally in the summer and knew the hut to be a snug base in the warm months, but it was proving just the opposite in winter. However, a roaring fire helped to change the atmosphere, and in the silly way of things we roared even louder when George left his shorts too near the blaze and had them disintegrate. However, with the legs cut off an old pair of pyjamas he made a dashing figure, and provided continual amusement for Bruce and myself whenever we looked at him.

There had been showers during the night and the river was up, so I knew that a crossing leading to the short cut across the toe of the Kinihi spurs through to Pannel Creek flats would be out of the question. This meant we would have to boulder-hop up-river, and after passing the Morse attempt a river crossing near the lower gorge.

With the weather as wretched as it was I was a bit concerned about the condition of the old Edison hut, which I knew to be in poor shape. Because of this prior knowledge we had replacement pots, and each of us carried some black plastic of heavy calibre to cover the roof in an effort to add a degree of snugness, as we had not really decided on the length of time we would stay in the valley. This would be decided by results.

Bruce Wright, one of my shooting companions in later years, who also spent some time shooting for Alpine Helicopters. He is shown loading chamois on to a truck at the base camp at Jacobs River.

The headwaters of the Edison. Photo taken from Barrier Cliff.

As we hiked up-stream the rain became heavier and the wind a few degrees colder, cutting through our oilskin coats and chilling the water flowing down our necks and out the armholes and through the legs of our shorts. The temperature was so low that snow and hail were inevitable before that day ended. Strangely, we managed the river crossing with little trouble, and leaving the bank we scrambled on to a plateau to the north and followed old blaze marks through the bush.

By the time we reached Pannel Creek we were soaked and frozen, but it was simply not on to stop for a spell. We had made good progress, just a little over two hours from the first hut to the top end of the Pannel Creek flats which, considering the weather and the weight of our packs, was really good going. But Bruce, who was still getting over a bout of tummy 'flu, looked ghastly, despite his protestations that he was "fit as a flea", and George and I determined to keep a weather eye on him. A quarter of an hour after crossing Pannel Creek we encountered snow, and as we pushed through the ferns and scrub snow began to stick to our faces. My hands had no feeling in them, and glancing behind I saw George with nose and lips a purplish colour, blowing the snow off his whiskers and eyebrows. Bruce, while keeping pace, was beginning to stumble, and he looked as white as the falling snow. In the end he was forced to stop and put his head between his knees, but we all realised that it was no time for stopping without facing the additional risks of exposure.

We were too far committed to go back, so we pumped Bruce full of glucose sweets and kept him tramping along with such encouraging white lies as, "the hut is just five or six minutes further on". The ruse worked — largely because Bruce wanted it to work, I believe — and after quite a number of "five minutes" the hut came in sight to provide us with our first good news of the trip. It was dry and snug, with a heap of firewood piled inside, and once we had used our plastic covers to proof the roof by tying them firmly over the flat iron, we soon had a fire and a feed to consolidate our new feeling of optimism.

Indeed, there was a pleasure in the warmth of that hut, just sitting listening to the pounding of the rain on the roof, deadened to some extent by the plastic, and the roar of the river rushing by some fifty yards or so below us. Clothes steamed in dampness before the fire, as the warmth forced out the cold from our bones. Even George risked drying his "pyjama" shorts.

Late in the afternoon the rain eased and then stopped, so while George completed his camp chores Bruce and I walked (in bush shirts and underpants) to the long slip behind the hut to see if there was game about. Bruce crossed to one side while I strolled up the centre and soon had the peepers on two deer feeding right in the path Bruce was following. I sat down on a large rock, and Bruce twigged that something was up when I began putting my hands over my eyes. He moved on until they came into view. The smaller of the pair, a young stag, looked round and returned to feeding, but the hind was more alert to danger and moved up the slip to the bush. We were content. We had not expected much game considering that it was winter, but the signs seemed to be good, and we hoped to get results with movie cameras and perhaps with rifles as well.

We drew straws that night to decide who would be first to rise and become firelighter and cook, a job hardly sought-after with the snow down to low levels and the temperatures hovering in sympathy. Bruce got the shortest straw, followed by George and myself — one occasion when being last man on the totem pole had advantages. None of us had brought a watch, and due to an oversight — mine — the transistor had been left back in the utility, so it meant that the timetable in the Edison hut was going to depend largely on guesswork. My first guess was that daylight would be around 7.30am.

It seemed I had hardly dropped off to sleep before Bruce had me shaken awake asking if we reckoned it was time to start getting ready. A daylight start meant rising in darkness, and from the warmth of my sleeping bag I seemed to see a tiny glimmer of light through the hut.

"Yeah. Better get up and get organised, Bruce," I said. So he stoked the fire, boiled the tea and got a large pan of sausages sizzling and giving off an aroma that grabbed at the nostrils.

However, once breakfast was over and we had drunk so many mugs of sweet tea that we seemed to be awash, it was still dark . . . just as dark as it had been when Bruce had started on the breakfast an hour earlier. So we snuggled

Rutting deer in the head of the Edison, a tributary of the Maitahi.

The old Edison hut, near the head of the Maitahi River. It was our base camp for meat-hunting between 1969 and 1972.

An earlier group of meat-shooters in the Pannell Creek area of the Maitahi, from the campsite alongside the airstrip that had just been built. *Left to right:* Brian Titheridge, "Popeye", Graham Allen (now a helicopter pilot) and Barry Petrie.

back into the down to await the dawn. When it finally arrived, we worked out that breakfast that morning must have been eaten around two o'clock.

George was keen to climb high behind the hut and sidle along beneath the sheer cliffs to a long, exposed spur about a mile up the valley. Bruce and I decided to travel up the west branch of the Edison valley and hop from one tributary to the next, returning to the valley floor via a high ridge I had observed during an earlier trip into the region.

The temperature was down where our spirits had been the day before, and the ground was frozen white. There was a chill wind whipping down the river to emphasise that water crossings were going to be very cold occasions that day. But at least there was no rain or sleet, and the fingers of light streaking through the tops of the range at the head of the valley offered the prospect that there would be sunlight and warmth later.

Bruce and I splashed out of the waist-high water afraid to stop once we got on to the bank in case we seized up like an old motor. It was impossible to tell if there was sign because the ground was covered with a fluffy coating of frost. Anyway, we kept going and managed to arrive on the snow tussock terraces at the same time as the sunlight, a happy augury.

Almost immediately we saw a chamois feeding on the edge of a shinglebank and decided to try stalking him, a task easier to contemplate than carry out. First, we climbed above the shingle before edging cautiously down to a decent vantage point. The stalk brought us to within less than twenty yards of the chamois and we were able to get some fine runs of movie film before Bruce decided to get some action material as well.

We tossed a rock at the buck to get him moving, but it moved on only a few paces and resumed feeding. It was not until we stood upright, waving our arms, that it took flight.

We decided there was no future in moving higher as the snow was too steep and no animal would bother living on it, so we moved east around the valley. Once into the very open bush we struck a lot of game sign and sighted four deer which ran only a short distance before stopping to peer back at us.

When we arrived at the next tributary we had a smoke while considering the prospects of following the stream to the basin above, and decided to chance our arms. It was a wise decision, for the way in was much more straightforward than it had looked from below, and at the lip of the basin we saw at once a group of chamois in a shallow snow-filled gully.

We managed to get above them and the movie cameras hummed as the chamois ploughed their way across our field of vision. And the buck leading the procession put on quite a performance: he would drive his two front legs down into the soft snow and at the same time give a shrill whistle. Bruce began to whistle back and this annoyed the buck no end. There were more chamois, but by this time we were fully engaged with a large flock of keas which surrounded us. The cheeky birds landed right at our feet, chewing our bootlaces and pecking at our socks. The more birds, the greater the din and the cheekier they got, until Bruce grabbed one of them and the whole flock went berserk. We were happy to leave them.

Later we climbed to the ridge I had hoped would lead us down to the Maitahi Valley floor, and struck a game trail which led us from clearing to clearing through a network of alpine scrub until we came to the tall timber. And then, as we were beginning to wind down ourselves, a stag burst out of the trees in front of us and we had to scramble madly in an effort to catch him side-on with the cameras. It was a highly satisfying day, and as we were joined at the hut by George within minutes of our own arrival we were able to kill the evening relating our minor adventures as the logs burned low.

George managed to gauge the time rather better than Bruce had done when he set about breakfast preparations, and it was barely light when we rinsed the plates and discussed the day's programme. George intended taking his rifle and climbing into the Edison Valley and working his way through the snow to the edge of the lake where Bruce and I had seen some goodlooking chamois bucks. For Bruce and myself the plan was to go up-river to the Mueller Pass and spend the day exploring the tributaries of the upper valley headwaters, our route to be a high-level one on the south side of the main river. By climbing high I knew we would get on to a terrace that would provide virtual flat-going to within half a mile or so of the open snowgrass in the valley. Planning was made easier because I had hunted that part of the valley from a helicopter and I knew virtually to within minutes how long it would take us to walk in.

But as on most such expeditions we had to cross the river, and chose a spot several hundred yards upstream from the hut. In winter conditions the water was so cold that my voice must have risen several octaves by the time we struggled on to dry land, but it was impossible to speak for a minute or so.

George left us at the Edison confluence, and Bruce and I began our climb beside a huge rock lying hard against the hillside. This brought us to my easy terrace where the ground was swampy and covered with a thick moss, as were the trees. Deer had stripped everything off the underscrub to a height of six feet or thereabouts, so it was possible to see for a considerable distance through the immediate vegetation. It was on this terrace that 90 per cent of all the deer in the upper valley lived, and we guessed that it was a bit over half a mile long and about half as wide -- at the most distant points.

Travel was easy across the springy moss covering of the terrace, and we were able to maintain a straight course by using a high, snowcapped peak at the head of the valley as a beacon. We came eventually to a dry overflow bed from the main river and followed this briefly before crossing to the north bank from where we were able to take an angle course to the top of a long shingle slip. Bruce and I then began a sidle which took us out to the open, snow-covered ground off the headwaters of the river. By using that terrace we had made the trip from hut door to headwaters in less than two hours!

The speed of our ascent meant that the sun was late clearing the peaks surround-

A female chamois and her kid, Morse River area. Note the female has only one horn.

A fine bull tahr, photographed below the head of the Mueller Pass, between the Maitahi and Zora Creek.

Climbing after tahr in the cliffs some 1,000 feet above above the Scone Creek region provided some hair-raising hunting.

ing us, and the early morning wind really whistled across the open ground. There were some chamois feeding on the edge of a glacier a few hundred yards from our resting place, and we took this as a good omen. We set up photographic gear and began a stalk towards them. For a time they seemed to participate in the game, but then trotted away up the far side of the glacier.

It had given the sun time to climb beyond the mountains, and across the far side of the valley a sun-drenched creek looked too appealing to pass up. We climbed off the end of the ice and began the trudge through the snow to the area of what might well have been named Golden Glow Creek, if it had a name at all. We went directly through an alpine scrub-covered spur instead of skirting it, and thus stumbled on one of the best bivouacs I had ever seen. It was bone-dry with an almost flat floor of sand, and there was an abundance of dry wood around the overhang. From inside it was possible to see virtually the complete valley floor, at least to the point where the trees began to thicken and the floor angled off steeply.

We crossed the river to the south bank, not without a great deal of bruising caused by slips from ice-covered boulders, and tramped up the edge of the shingle fan to the sunny crags above. There was an abundance of deer sign, and a minimum of skill would have been required to move into the surrounding bush and bop an animal or two. But our first interest was shooting film. The absent George was the eager hunter on this trip.

But as Bruce and I clambered to the top of the shingle fan we saw the opening of a narrow canyon which, on inspection, contained eight chamois. One was a large buck, so we decided that I should stalk up close and shoot it with a small, light-weight "takedown" rifle and silencer we had along, while Bruce photographed the whole manoeuvre. I had covered about a dozen yards or so when Bruce whistled and pointed to a chamois standing perhaps thirty yards, away with just his head showing over the top of a clump of tussock. However, it had only a small head of horns so I decided to ignore it and seek the chosen victim, still feeding with several other chamois.

When I reached the lip of a huge piece of shale I motioned over my shoulder to Bruce that the "kill" was on, so I stood up. I put the narrow sniper scope's cross-hair on the buck, and his crumpling action seemed to coincide with the muffled *plop* of the rifle's report. Bruce gave me the thumb's-up sign, and we were about to walk across to the fallen buck when another group of chamois appeared further up the canyon. And then others. Animals to the left of us, animals to the right of us . . .

Moving up through the snow I met an ice barrier which forced me to climb wide and higher to bypass it, and while gathering breath after the exertion I saw a tahr staring at me from fifty or so yards away. And behind the tahr were more chamois, about eight of them, with a group of tahr standing behind them! I searched around desperately for Bruce, but he was way back of beyond, enjoying the sun as he prepared lunch, and the camera gear lay beside him. I looked helplessly at the animals and they looked, helplessly I guess, at me. Stalemate!

Mumbling curses in my best imprecatory manner at Bruce Wright's favour of food over filming, I scrambled back down through the snow to join him at lunch. It was remarkable, really, considering all the helicopter activity in such an open area that we were able to see so many animals. Bruce returned with me to have a look at the tahr, which had moved on to a higher ridge, before returning to deal with the chamois I had shot earlier. It took a few minutes to remove the headskin before we made our way down the valley.

A chamois appeared and moved ghostlike along the base of the cliffs in a line parallel to the one we were travelling, and then disappeared. As we gained the tall timber in the lip of the basin the deer sign increased, and we were hardly surprised to see four deer on the far side of a wide, dry wash. I halted so quickly that Bruce, close behind, almost pushed me into the deep wash. He handed over the rifle, took a firm grasp to steady me as I leaned against the side of a tree over the edge of the bank and fired. Daylight was on the wane, so we took what venison we needed, plus an excellent pelt, and resumed the journey back to camp. George was ready with a fire roaring and a story of derring-do and success in hunting chamois, so we were well satisfied with our trip into the Maitahi.

But George was really after a tahr, a big fellow with the potential to win a competition trophy in his local branch of the Deerstalkers' Association in Central Otago. Time was running out for George; he had to get back to the farm at Wedderburn, while Bruce and I had time to spare. It was merely a matter of deciding which river we should move on to for the most likely result, and the Scone Creek region won the day. So it was back to civilisation to restock supplies and on to the big tahr.

We knew that Jim Wilson, a fine pilot-mechanic with an air force background, was flying a helicopter up the Whataroa River on meat recovery so we thumbed a ride with him into Scone Creek. While George and Bruce flew in on the first trip, I helped pay our way by assisting the ground "gutter" clean and drag a new load of tahr carcases into a line ready for collection. Jim dropped the boys off at the Scone hut and, after collecting another load of tahr from the gut heap near the Hughes Basin, returned with these before flying me in as well. By the time I got to the Scone the hut was organised and a brew was ready. Jim Wilson pointed out for us an area where he had seen tahr, so the next morning George was hotfoot into it, while Bruce and I opted to do axe work on the track leading up to the Scone Basin, and erect rock piles up the creekbed itself. These stone piles, pyramid-shaped, were designed to indicate the best route bypassing obstacles such as waterfalls and boulders. As so often happens, we were working upstream after leaving the bush when we saw a rather large mob of tahr on a high exposed ridge between the Upper Scone and Bettison Stream. If we had been hunting, instead of doing trackwork, the tahr would probably have been somewhere else, but the opportunity was too good to miss, so our next day's operation was decided on the spot.

Back at the hut George reported having seen plenty of tahr, but ice conditions had been so severe he had refused to shoot animals in range because of the virtual

The impressive Bettison Stream region.

impossibility of retrieving them. All the tahr he had seen were on a very exposed ridge and had obviously gained their lofty perch — it could hardly be described as much else — from an ascent route further along the main ridge. We told him of our own sightings, and that we believed it would be possible to reach the animals we had observed.

I got off before Bruce and George the next morning and set the movie gear up to film them as they emerged from the bush and boulder-hopped towards me. It was then upstream to the base of a steep spur that Bruce and I had selected as our route to the first snowfields. It was obvious we had a tough climb in prospect, and the amount of snow showing through the open patches of lower bush suggested it would be a cold one as well, at least until we escaped from the vegetation into the open.

That alpine scrub proved a veritable curse. We were forced at times to worm our way forward beneath it to make any progress at all, and then to scramble over the top of it as best we might. And then, when we finally broke clear, we discovered our route had brought us to a near-vertical cliff that offered particular problems with its ice-encrusted flat rocks. We decided to risk it in the hope that it would taper off in gradient the higher we climbed, and as I led with Bruce at No. 2 I could hear George muttering about "a bloody suicidal outfit", and that instead of "hunting with Harker" it looked as though it might be a case of "dying with Harker".

George Lindsay gutting his tahr while helicopter pilot and and good samaritan Jim Wilson watches.

I could tell from this that my mates were in great form. We moved ahead. Bruce added his pennyworth by suggesting in fun that with any luck we would be leaning out backwards in the best mountain-climbing tradition . . . or at least the way they showed it on the telly. He was to be near the mark, too.

We thought the first bluff was rough enough, but the next was far worse. It was possible to see the bloke behind simply by looking straight down at your feet! Finally, however, I managed to claw my way up to a steep icefield and gain the edge of a pointed rock where I could wait in relative comfort and safety until Bruce clambered up beside me. About sixty yards away a group of tahr, five of them, stood watching our antics. One was a young male not yet sporting a mane; the remainder were females. Eventually they moved off and were lost to our sight behind a high reef of jagged rock protruding from the snow.

We climbed up through the icefield for some way until arriving at a deadend from which we might have managed to proceed if we'd had crampons, an ice axe and ropes with us. So we had either to cross the narrow icefield or go back — and the latter was impossible. But the ice crossing was no cakewalk either, for it was steep and offered all manner of hazard.

However, we made it safely, and from our new vantage point could see quite plainly tahr of all shapes and sizes standing on a ridge some 450 yards away. But the distance between our two points of vantage read like an obstacle course with tragic penalties for anyone who made a single serious error of judgment. There were deep, ice-filled chasms, valleys where rock-hard snow had fallen hundreds of feet below, and vertical bluffs offering a minimum of help in the way of cracks for hand or footholds.

First some movie film of the region, then it was on with the motley. Bruce had an old rifle with a solid butt-plate, and used this to smash the ice to gain footholds. A slip on the steep face spelt certain disaster, probably death, yet we never thought in these terms at the time. It was only later, when going over the trips in my mind, that I realised some of the appalling risks.

Progress was slow and careful. Bruce smashed the ice, I held him firmly by his shirt-tail after settling my feet firmly in the ice holes he cut with the rifle butt, and in this way we made our crossing to the middle of the field. We had stopped for a breather when snow and ice began spilling down from high above us.

Our pounding on the ice had started the snow moving above us, and we realised quickly enough that if it all began to slip we were goners. We were literally frozen to the spot with terror. Luck was along with us that day, and the snow gathered no momentum, and we moved more quickly and with less pounding for the second half of the crossing.

Once over the ice we faced a high climb, and the whole time several tahr stood watching us, like sentinels posted to warn of attack from below. Perhaps they did not issue that warning because they regarded our likelihood of a successful ascent so lightly, and as I remember George Lindsay, who was last man in the shirt-tail brigade, tended to agree with them. However, we finally managed to gain the base of a narrow crack in a rock wall which seemed to lead up and on to a high plateau of snow. We followed it up and, just as I started to stand straight at the plateau's edge, I spotted a mob of tahr standing on a bench of protruding granite.

A quick pow-wow with the lads, and I set up the camera while they set about preparing their rifles and choosing targets. The tahr were perhaps 60 yards from us, milling around and seemingly unaware of the danger so close to them despite all their activity. I pushed the camera button and nodded to the gunmen.

Both rifles went off together. The big bull tahr George had fired at staggered, but managed to run with the herd until they reached a near-vertical ridge overlooking a valley of ice that sloped steeply down to a sheer cliff.

The old fellow stumbled and fell head first over the slope to the valley below. Gathering momentum on the frozen surface he sped on to the edge of the cliff and catapulted over. About thirty tahr moved into sight above us, but there would have been little chance of an accurate shot for they were literally flying over the snow.

So we pinpointed the spot where George's big tahr had gone over and decided to retrieve it later in the week by helicopter. In the near-freezing conditions there was no chance of the carcass "going off" as it were. From our own point of view, the task was to get off the tops which had proved so difficult to get on to in the first place. However, we finally struck a ridge, after a number of frustratingly unsuccessful dabs at other areas, which offered sufficient handholds to take us towards a welcome shingle slip snaking down to the valley floor. This proved something of a morale booster, I can tell you.

So it was back to the hut to await the arrival of Jim Wilson and his helicopter. We were able to find George's tahr without much trouble, for the old fellow had come to rest near the edge of a glacier and George had little trouble securing him beneath the chopper for the flight out of the valley to the utility.

If ever there was an illustration of the advantage to hunters of helicopters, that was it. George would have lost that trophy if we had not been able to call on Jim Wilson's assistance, but as it was he got the reward of some very hard climbing — a real hunter's reward.

CHAPTER NINE

THEY WENT THATAWAY

HUNTING is a very serious business for some people, and there is no doubt that it has its serious aspects, especially those with regard to safety. But for me the great pleasure in hunting on the Coast was the tremendous range of characters I was able to meet and to hunt with, and the trips I most enjoyed were those which produced the biggest laughs. In fairness to some of my companions, I must admit that the humour of the situation did not always strike me at the time, but looking back on some of those experiences, with time rubbing the rough patches off, I can regard them now as absolutely hilarious.

Early in 1972 I was planning a shoot up the Morse River when my old mate Ernie Wilson arrived with a burst of enthusiasm and permission to hunt some property up the Arahura River. The way he told it, the stags in this particular region must have been crossed with elephants at some time because they were HUGE! And I should have known the whole project had its foundations built on shifting sands when Ernie came up with his clinching argument: the place at which we would stay could be reached by car and there was an automatic electricity plant for lighting and heating. It all sounded too good to be true, but perhaps I was wanting to be convinced. Anyway I changed my plans about the Morse River project and opted to join Ernie. The expedition had a rough start when his car ran out of petrol outside the Lake Mahinapua Hotel. The early start was abandoned for a lunchtime beginning, and we took off up a side-road from the access highway around Lake Kaniere,

The irrepressible Ernie Wilson beats the heat in an ice-fed stream.

ending up in a farmyard which we shared with a big, old bull. Fortunately, he seemed content to keep his distance.

The surrounding valley floor appeared to offer great deer country, and was rather like a small-scale Arawata or Landsborough River, with grassy flats sloping up to the bush edge, and various side creeks fringed fairly thickly with toetoes. The amount of food available to deer was plentiful, so game in the region should be in great condition.

This, it seemed, was it. Ernie decided to take one area while I went through another, and we set a time and place to return for a meeting at dusk four hours later. Despite a close sweep of the valley floor and along the bush edge I came across only a few old hoofprints and some tinder-dry droppings. This must be a slack part of the valley, I opined. The main interest of my stalk was the discovery of an abandoned mine shaft dug into a creek wall, with the mess of old iron that seems to be the companion of such places. When Ernie appeared he had little more to report than I: two or three hoofprints in some sand beside a creek, and these appeared to have been made by a young deer.

Back at the farmhouse we had a brew of tea and decided to use the dark to advantage by trying out the spotlight. We drove a mile or so to an old track which had been used for dragging logs out of the bush, and set off along it on foot seeking the deer Ernie assured me were in the region. We walked the length of the track. Midnight came without a single sighting, and when drizzle looked as though it would set in we decided to make tracks for the car and give the hunting best. As we walked we flashed the spot against the bush edge and saw two weasels chasing something through the grass. Almost together Ernie and I spoke of how cruel these animals were, and the vicious damage they inflicted on birdlife, so when one of them ran out on to the road we acted in concert. Ernie kept the light on the weasel while I sighted the two saphire-like eyes in the rifle's scope and eased on the trigger at about ten yards. The weasel almost disintegrated under the blow of the heavy .308 bullet, but Ernie and I felt better for some reason.

When we returned to the old farmhouse Ernie added too much water to the stew and it emerged as thick soup, but after the sort of day it had been, neither of us seemed to care too much. We later decided that spotlighting south of Ross offered the best hope - perhaps our only hope - of game for the final day of the week so the following day we erected a special iron frame on Ernie's car. It had been designed by the maestro himself, and could be bolted to the roof of his vehicle with comparative ease. The platform enabled the shooter to be at a height of almost twelve feet when standing upright, and allowed the spotlight to shine over gorse and scrub that would be an obstruction at normal shooting levels.

So we went out that night along an old logging track behind Lake Ianthe armed with a .270 rifle and two powerful lights, cruising slowly along the old log track, with Ernie handling the driving. When three sets of eyes suddenly glowed in the darkness, reflecting the light, I tapped on the car roof with my foot. Ernie's head appeared out the window, and I motioned him to reverse a few yards. There, sure

One of the successful ventures with Ernie, producing seven deer from two clearings in the Karangarua. We called in Goodwin McNutt's helicopter to take the catch back out to the roadway.

enough, stood a stag and two hinds in the tangle of bush and scrub, about eighty or so yards from the car. I took a resting shot and a pair of eyes "went out". The remaining deer disappeared in different directions, so we abandoned the vehicle and, with a battery light, took off in pursuit through the swamp heavily trapped with logs in various conditions of decay.

Ernie carried the light, and scrambled along an upturned tree to gain some height for a sweep around the area. I inched my way carefully behind him, for the log was moving and one had to adjust to the rocking movement to maintain balance. Ernie flashed the light, and a set of eyes were illuminated.

"Hurry up and shoot the damned thing," he hissed. But it was easier said than done from my rocky position standing behind him. So I rested the barrel on his head, took aim at the illuminated eyes and fired. A large stag lurched from the bracken and fell kicking about on the ground.

At that same instant the top end of the tree on which we were balanced groaned once and broke away, and Ernie and I tumbled about four yards into the bog. It was a case of real panic stations as we floundered close enough to where the unfortunate stag had kicked its last a few seconds earlier. We got the stag, the sole return from our hunt, but we looked like a couple of escapees from a horror movie.

Whenever that laugh show *Dad's Army* appears on television my mind seems automatically to click on to Benny Davies, one of the earliest hunting companions I had on the Coast, and our experiences flash through behind the old eyes like an ancient movie replay. Despite the years, I can still recall the first trip (1968) we actually went on together, and it was a classic of its kind. True, we nearly came to fisticuffs, but it nevertheless stands out as one of the funniest hunting expeditions in my memory. Indeed, on the occasions on which I saw Ben later — 1971 was probably the last — we tended to hash the old experiences over and garnish them a

Time for fun in the old flying fox up the Wanganui. After three hours of working on the wreck, Paul Bevernage, who never seemed to suffer from nerves, was the first willing passenger to cross the river in our transport repaired with bindertwine and fencing wire.

Yet another way of moving a carcase. Pat York manoeuvres a large stag tied to a truck inner-tube for floating downstream.

bit, and enjoy them more and more with each retelling, in the way of hunters. But I shall try and give the facts without too much fiction.

Ben had arrived at my place from Napier in a borrowed Land Rover which had seen better days and gave every impression it would hardly last long enough to see worse. The sound was bad, and each mile was a large step towards total collapse. I was much younger then, much less experienced, and eager to make my way in the hunting business. I suggested to Ben that perhaps we should take my car, but he would have none of it.

"Besides," he declared, "in this sort of wagon you really look the part."

So like the two Great White Hunters off to the jungle to save the village from the tiger, we left Ross in what might reasonably be termed "a puff of smoke". We made surprisingly good time, and were probably saved from suffocation from the exhaust fumes permeating the vehicle by the gale which deviated through every ripped seam of the canvas top. Twenty or so miles on and a terrible grinding beneath the chassis suggested the need for a comfort stop for the vehicle, not us. The exhaust pipe had finally come adrift and was twisted to such an extent that further persistence with it was of little avail. Ben simply ripped it right out and tossed it over a bank.

Besides "looking the part", we now sounded the part as well.

Our objective was the Paringa River, but with the fumes situation much worsened by the loss of the muffler and pipe, the radiator boiling, and the motor missing and coughing like a bad case of bronchitis every time we limped up a hill, there had to be agreement that our chances of reaching that destination were lessening drastically with every mile. We stopped at Whataroa to review our circumstances over a cool beer and decided that an attempt to reach Fox Glacier and get a shot in the Cook River region was probably as ambitious as we should reasonably become. That was where we aimed, and that was where we eventually got — at 3pm. and after a puncture in the baldest of four bald tyres. It had taken eight hours for a journey of eighty five miles.

Still, as Ben had said, we looked the part.

Early next morning, armed with permits and guns, we were off upriver on the north bank, and turned up the very first creek, just a few hundred yards above the road bridge. The creek, which was for the first part dry, led almost to the snow tussock, and within a couple of hours we were standing at the edge of a shingle wash looking up at the nearby tops. We had made better time on foot, it seemed, than in Ben's jalopy.

So we climbed into the tops with high optimism. Nothing. In those days there was no helicopter pressure in the Cook area, and we had rather confidently expected to find any number of chamois bounding hither and yon. Still, the day was young, so we decided to pitch our tent, get rid of our encumbering packs and cover a lot of country during the light hours.

The first problem arose almost immediately. The tent was a pole tent, so we had to find poles. I had suggested at Ross bringing my pup tent, but Ben would have none of it: "Hell, man. I like to move round a bit; we'll take mine." So I had meekly bowed to Ben's wishes and left my tent.

And I can say that we did "move round" all right. We covered a lot of ground just looking for a depression in which to pitch the tent so the ropes could be drawn straight out. Eventually, we found a hole big enough in which to put the tent, and built a large rock cairn at one end to which to anchor the main guy rope.

What we needed after that was a good brew of tea to get the chins back up again, but the efficient Harker had left the fuel for the white-spirit cooker back in the vehicle. Any idea how long it takes to boil the billy over a grass fire? By this time our grins and "looking the part" had slipped away, but we finally managed to get hunting. The shooting improved the further we went and it became a competition as to who would get the next chamois. In those early days neither Ben nor I was interested in trophies, so a head was either a "biggie" or a "little 'un". We kept going at a good clip, shooting whatever appeared until we realised just how far we had travelled, how low the sun had gone -- and how far we had to go back.

I favoured going back the way we had come, but Ben considered that if we were to "tear round this knob, and thunder through this gap, then duck over this ridge" we would halve the return tramping time. It seemed to my relatively inexperienced eye that Ben's route contained rather a lot of gullies which would make "thundering through the gaps" a pretty long business, but he had done the more hunting, and I bowed to his experience.

After an hour I was in the mood to have shot him. There seemed to be an unending series of gullies up which we had to make our way, a great shortage of gaps to

Caught feeding: two female chamois photographed in the head of the Tuke.

thunder through and a multitude of ridges which made ducking impossible and hard slog inevitable. I was bushed, and the pecker was down a bit as I considered the chances of getting back to the tent that night very remote indeed. It was getting darker by the minute, and only the beautiful crystal-clear sky prolonged the twilight.

I had to call a halt. I used the excuse of needing a smoke, but what I needed more was rest and reassurance. Ben sat beside me, chipper as ever, smoking his pipe.

"Not far now, boy," he declared with the assurance of the Great White Hunter. "Just bolt over there" -- he waved an expansive arm across half the mountains of South Westland -- "and nip down that gully and we're there."

I smoked quietly, seething. I looked back up the hill to see how far we had come, and just over a crest near a spur I spied the cairn we had built to provide some stabilisation for the tent. I suppressed my first inclination to shout the good news, and let revenge submerge that feeling of goodwill.

"Come on, Ben. Where the hell is the tent?" I demanded.

He grabbed a bit of stick and drew an elaborate series of spirals on the ground with ridges, spurs, tarns and almost every other distinguishing feature of mountain terrain. We'd have had trouble travelling so far, even with the Land Rover operative. But it was an impressive map — and an impressively confident performance.

When I applied the cruncher by suggesting that it might be easier all round if we strolled the eighty or so yards to the tent behind us, Ben stood up and declared that it simply could *not* be our tent. However, we spent the night in it, in sleeping bags identical to the ones we had packed up the mountainside, and the rest of the gear gave every appearance of being exact copies of our own stuff.

For some obscure reason, the next day went off without a hitch and we had a magnificent day hunting chamois over a wide area. It seemed to recharge Ben's confidence, and he was determined to take a new route off the tops by way of a spur that seemed to ramble down almost to the road bridge.

Two deer with one shot from a Mauser 66. The author saw one deer feeding on the edge of the clearing and shot it through the neck, but when he walked over he found another deer lying in the bracken behind it. This was in the Hitchen Basin above Isobel Falls.

Meat hunting during the summer months held many heart-aches. Here Barry Petrie picks blowfly eggs and maggots out of a stag while waiting for the helicopter to come in and collect our load.

Picking a route through the Glacier was like walking through a maze. A number of the icicle pinnacles were eight to ten times taller than a man.

But I had learned a lesson up on the tops which was to stand me in good stead in the hunting years which followed, so I really owed Ben a lot. We went down from the tops my way. It was a great personal sadness when I learned in 1973 that Ben had been killed in a road accident.

Besides the laughs there were other memorable occasions which provided conversational fodder for those nights on the tops crammed into tents or sprawled around the hut fires. One that was always sure to spark off a virtual fireworks of speculation was my recollection of a 1968 expedition undertaken with Barry Petrie and Pete Billington when we sought an acceptable ascent route on to the ridge overlooking Whirling Water. We were then to head south-east towards a large basin lying between the steep snowtopped mountains. The terrain which drops from this ridge is amongst the worst New Zealand can offer, but we did not know it at the time.

The first stage of the journey was easy work across riverflat to a Forest Service hut, and we pushed it fairly hard, thus allowing time to secure permanent ropes up and across Morgan Stream to assist hunting parties in heavy rain or flood conditions. The next day offered a chance to test the high country, so we waded through Whirling Water and headed downstream to where the bush track enters the lower end of the flat. Through the open forest and on to the spur, which lay to the south side of the first stream encountered before the flats, we walked on for about twenty minutes before dropping into the stream. We then took the north spur, veered south-east towards a long ridge and found it was a continuation of the high country we planned to reach. Passage through the low-lying forest was easy until we reached the subalpine fringe, and then we really had to work. Bad weather made the trip something of a nightmare, and the descent required a lot of fingertip work, edging along vertical terrain while gazing between our boots at the narrow twisting creek 300 feet below. It was heaven to get back to the hut.

But the part of the trip which was to prove even more interesting as a conversational piece than the rugged country was a sighting Barrie Petrie and I made when we were heading upstream one day to stalk the Fivefinger and Broadleaf covey that braces the far side of the foaming Waitaha. Barry was ahead and I saw him stop and tense.

Following his gaze I saw a cream-coloured hind feeding at the mouth of a creek outlet. For nearly two minutes we watched her every movement until she became lost from sight in the bracken. I did not learn if the beautiful animal was ever shot, but I hope she was not. Previous to that particular visit, perhaps a month or so earlier, I had shot a stag in the vicinity and he had cream head markings, so the likelihood was that there were other piebalds in the region. Genetic freak that hind might have been, but she was a really fine looking animal.

Tony Charles was hunting in the Macquarie River territory in Australia when he ran into a fellow who had been out hunting chamois with me in South Westland, and during conversation the Aussie had provided my address in Ross. I had a note from Tony ("What I want is a reasonable stag") but the man himself proved something of a surprise: he topped my six feet by four inches, and his mop of unruly red hair was matched by a bushy beard of the same hue. The weather late in the year was proving unpredictable, so I decided to take him and try Miserable Ridge which tended to miss a lot of the lowflying cloud. Access was straightforward, following the Mikonui upstream from the first flat before the Tuke and Dickson rivers. By staying on the north bank of the Mikonui, we made progress upstream past the two tributaries until the surrounding mountain sides squeezed the river into a narrow though still accessible race. Once into the narrows we followed the track upstream until we came to the access track to Explorer Hut. We took the path pointing towards the hut and made shelter within twenty minutes.

The next day was dull, with high cloud and high humidity, and as we tramped into the alpine fringe the birdlife of the region was in full chorus and provided a background of sound as we moved on to the snowgrass. I used the glasses to inspect the series of narrow guts that ran from the confronting spur and parallel to where we were resting. The guts with their steep sides had a handsome crop of mountain carrot, that delicacy much sought after by game in the high pastures. We saw some hinds, but there were no stags visible.

So I outlined my plan to Tony. He was fit and experienced, so I had no doubts that he would be able to handle the scheme I had in mind. We would head south along Miserable Ridge towards Mt Bowen, where there was some really rough and difficult country to get through, to a great little grassy basin tucked away near an unnamed creek. It was an area which, because of the difficulties of access, was likely to be a great producer of game opportunities.

Tony was keen, so off we went. I strung some toilet paper around the shrubs near the track entrance, much to his astonishment, but I explained that the white paper would make a vivid contrast against the dark green foliage, and that strips hung in strategic places served as marvellous track guides in unfamiliar country. Anyone caught in the darkness would appreciate particularly the usefulness of the paper guide, and as I explained to Tony, the likelihood was that darkness would find us high on the snowgrass, but my torch and the paper markers would light the way home for us. It was cheap insurance as far as I was concerned.

While heading along the mountainside we stumbled on to an old campsite constructed from the flat slabs of shale found in the vicinity. It was well made and well concealed in a small depression, and it must have occupied many man-hours. Tucked into the base of one wall was a bottle containing a faded note, but two names were legible: Malcolm Dunn, Napier, 1951; and Ed Wells, Tauranga, 1951. If they were among the builders, then they can take some pleasure from the knowledge that it lasted a couple of decades.

We continued on to the lip of the creek-head, and it was hard work. My mate was panting like a traction engine, and the best recovery medicine I could think of was some game, so I swept the far spur with the glasses. My warning cry that it looked

Barry Petrie and I worked this country systematically, looking for tahr when we were getting up to $15 for top-quality headskins. Photograph shows the entrance of Prospectors Creek, Perth River.

as though I had a goodish stag lined up in the binoculars soon had Tony on his feet. I laid out a stalk pattern which would bring him to within 150 yards of the grazing stag, on his uphill side. Tony was using a .280 Remington, so a shot of this distance would be child's play. But he refused to move further. He gave me a full piece on bullet trajectories and velocities which added up to an argument that he could bowl the stag from where he was. He went ahead and prepared for the shot, missing badly with the first couple, which ended up below the stag in the hillside.

I chuckled. He swore. The distance was around 700 yards, so it didn't surprise me that the stag seemed unmoved by Tony's gunmanship. It moved around the shoulder of spur and was lost to view.

There was only one thing to do, so I motioned Tony to follow as I ran helter-skelter around the edge of the basin until we got behind a boulder with a new angle on the stag and a shot of perhaps 200 yards. This time there was no mistake. As the gunshot rang around the basin, the stag reared and fell.

But a glance at the sun dipping towards the Tasman gave emphasis to my urgings that we should get on to the journey homeward to the hut. By the time the sun finally fell into the sea we were using the torch and following my paper trail, which demonstrated its worth. Tony's stag head is a showpiece in an Auckland sports goods shop, and whenever I have written to Tony I always make a point of heading the letter up . . . . . LONG SHOT.

There are the occasional fluke shots which become something of a legend in hunting circles, and a conversational piece in any company. While I was chasing a fairly large herd of chamois down the mountainside to Robinson's Slip I saw a shot I have never seen repeated. Sitting on an outcrop of snowgrass with my legs dangling over a large rock slide I could see two Australian hunters steadily forcing chamois down a narrow rock defile which dropped away to a sheer drop. When they finished shooting they joined me and I was able to point out to them a white speck across the farthest side of the mighty slip basin. It looked to the naked eye like a white beetle, but through the binoculars it was a large billygoat, though even magnified it took time to find the old chap.

Paul Tarlington, a New South Welshman, had a look and began immediately to prepare his 'scope for a shot. I was too amazed to laugh. The distance across the slip face was more than half a mile and the goat was, in my judgment, threequarters of the way across. Paul asked me to provide the trajectory through the binoculars, and I reported his first shot fifty feet low. His second had the right elevation but was to the left. The goat was completely bewildered and ran around on his high rocky ledge.

As the next shot barked in my ear I counted the slow second through the lens as the bullet reached out across the slip and dropped the goat. The 303/270 bullet drove home, and a fantastic shot was recorded. It was a fluke, yet Paul could claim he set it up, and that he'd had a couple of ranging shots before his successful one.

Joseph Janowski, of the ASA, saw the shot besides myself, so it was not a case of pulling a longbow. It happened all right.

But let me finish this section of stories the way I started - with my old mate Ernie Wilson. He talked me into going into the Arahura River area with him when I had planned to go into the Morse River region, so a few weeks after that comedy of errors I encouraged him to accompany me on my originally planned trip. On this occasion we were joined by three others from Christchurch, including Trevor Lister and Bruce Wright, and they had to be fit, as we found it necessary to jog at times to make the Maitahi River hut before darkness, because of our late start.

Despite this seeming lack of organisation at so early a stage of the expedition, it was a wholly serious business on which we were engaged. Ernie, Trev and a mate were going to explore a high plateau in a hanging basin below Mt Kinihi on the Bannock Brae Range, while my own interest was the Morse region. However, the final part of the trip in was made in darkness due to spotlighting on the way up the valley and there was a considerable amount of stumbling around by the party of five before we emerged from the bush and on to the bottom of a large flat. Ahead was the hut, with a soft glow of light from the windows indicating it was occupied.

I led the way in, pushing open the door and ready to hail some rough hunters only to find a chap and a girl sitting at the table. Just which lot, occupants or visitors, got the biggest surprise is rather difficult to judge, but in a more subtle sense I felt there might have been a shade of disappointment accompanying our arrival. It made me think the couple were honeymooners, but they didn't say, and we didn't ask.

However, when I first burst through the door, the crush from my companions behind was hard to resist, so I stepped aside to enable more of them to enter. And in came Ernie, typically. The young woman had a string of frilly underclothes hung across the room drying. Ernie, intent on getting rid of his pack, bumped into the line and brought it down, draping the dainty pieces around his shoulders and getting the clasp of a bright red under-garment caught in his hair.

The situation was not aided by the chortles of the younger members of our party, and by the time Ernie had blundered from beneath the string of "smalls" the couple had decided to vacate the hut and set up house in a pup tent. Poor old Ernie wasn't allowed to forget that performance too quickly . . .

CHAPTER TEN

ON SAFARI

GUIDING TROPHY-HUNTERS was a wonderful way to meet the world in South Westland. But it had its problems, largely because the guide was expected to nursemaid the clients. Usually, the safaris were arranged before there was any opportunity to vet the prospective hunters to ensure that they were compatible or, more importantly, to see if they were fit enough to handle the conditions experienced on the Coast. Generally, it was easier to take New Zealand hunters into the bush or up to the alpine levels than it was for those from abroad, for the Kiwi at least had some idea of the sort of conditions he would be likely to face. In the main, the Kiwi who sought a guide was a reasonably experienced hunter, and not just a wallet seeking a head for the wall of the den.

In the case of some overseas visitors, it seems that they had read of the good trophies available in New Zealand, and a quick safari offered a chance for some one-upmanship on their clubmates back home.

Money was no barrier to these fellows, and I used to charge them $50 a day guiding fees, plus helicopter hire. Add their fares across the Tasman or the Pacific and they were paying big money for their pleasures. For instance, a piston-engined chopper cost $180 an hour, the jet FH1100 four-seater $200 an hour, and the Hughes 500 was $220 an hour.

The helicopter charges were constant for all hunters, of course, be they American or Abyssinian, but my own charges varied according to what the market would bear. New Zealanders were charged $15 a day; Australians $25 a day and so on. The Kiwis got my services on the cheap because that was all they were willing to pay! In the main they'd prefer a do-it-yourself hunting safari if charges in the overseas range were mentioned, so I had to tailor the fees to suit the client. Usually, I hired Goodwin McNutt's helicopter, but over a period I utilised most of the companies operating on the Coast.

The American hunters (or trophy seekers) were generally likeable fellows, sincere and usually affable, who knew what they wanted. Once they achieved what they had come for, rifles were set aside and out came the cameras. They never killed merely for the sake of it. All the Americans I met were excellent sportsmen.

Typical of this breed were Tes Zonneveld and Marty Gilliam of New Jersey. We took them by an old Hiller 12E chopper to the head of the Whataroa and pitched a tent in an area where there is now a hut available. Both visitors were using a new

Englishman Jim McEwan's stag, shot in the County Stream region. It measured 39" by 39½" (990.6 mm x 1003.3 mm).

type of automatic rifle, the .30-06 Kreighoff, which I had not seen until that time, and both of them were excellent shots. However, as soon as they had achieved in the field the trophies they had come out to get they set aside their weapons and did the rest of their shooting on film. Both men, strangely, had a dislike of heights, but as they were keen to get tahr it meant I had to place them strategically in the top country. Neither had spent much time roughing it in tents, but they became enthusiasts for living out and using spirit cookers.

An Englishman, James McEwan, of Brighton, made no bones about the fact that all he had previously shot was a duck, and even then he had a feeling the bird had had a death-wish and had flown deliberately into a pattern of shot. However, by taking things slowly we managed to get Jim safely into Kiwi Flat on our first day out from civilisation, and then moved on to the confluence of the Waitaha with the County Stream for our second night, walking to the head of the Stream the following day. I remember particularly that as we left the alpine scrub a large stag appeared about fifty yards ahead and Jim loosed a volley of shots which chipped the rocks, shook the trees and finallly took the stag in the shoulder. Once the stag went down, he was satisfied. He was happy then to leave and return to the coast; he had achieved what he had come for. I explained that we still had four days to go and could probably get a chamois and, if he was really lucky, perhaps a tahr as well.

Jim was no outdoors man. He couldn't put up a tent or cook, or really do any of those camp chores which the Kiwi hunter seems to be brought up to do. Indeed, I found it was easier for me to get him settled on a nearby rock, cleaning a rifle magazine or the like, while I got on and did the chores myself. However, I had to emphasise how important each of these tasks was to the expedition, because he was so eager to make his full contribution, and would have been most upset to feel he was doing less than his share. But in three days he had cleaned me out of ammunition — though he had five chamois to show for his efforts. Although none of the animals was of trophy standard, the pelts were in first class order, and he was eager to get back to England with his goodies and his tales of derring-do.

Chamois aplenty, and Lewis Rukavina took his share.

Each and every safari was an education in its way. Early in 1972 Teddy Rowlands phoned from Melbourne seeking a couple of weeks on chamois, and though I urged the use of a helicopter to get into the back country, he reckoned there was plenty of time and preferred to walk. As it turned out, he was totally unfit for the rigours of the Coast hunting country and I began to worry about his welfare. The further we went into the bush the more gear I collected, until I looked like a packhorse, loaded with just about everything but his rifle.

However, Teddy shot a fine 11-point stag, a terrific trophy, and five chamois with horn lengths exceeding 10 inches, the longest being 10⅝ inches (269.88mm). My fears that he might turn out to be a difficult companion were groundless. He proved to be a keen hunter and a cooperative and generous bloke — even though he set fire to my sleeping bag! While doing the chores he filled the cooker with white spirit and some of it must have spilled on my sleeping bag, for when the cooker was lit (a good foot away from the bag) there was a *woooff* and Harker's pride and joy burst into flames.

A few miles north of the Karangarua River is the Havelock Stream, so unimpressive that it seldom warrants a glance . . . just a gushing thread of water, but a route as well to the steep slopes of Mt Myers and, more important, Ryan's Peak. But it is a route that I discovered the really hard way — and one I would recommend only to someone to whom I owed a bad turn! However, when I used it the first time early in 1969 I was taking Lewis Rukavina in for chamois and it turned out to be one of the toughest trips I had made, especially the top half-mile of the Havelock.

The early stages of the creek are plain sailing, and tend to fudge what is awaiting the unwary further up. I had shot the region several years earlier with the McClausland brothers and Steve Johnson, so the general topography was familiar to me. But I simply did not expect so many narrow gorges and slime-covered bluffs

A deer which walked to its death by passing a clump of ferns in which the author was resting.

This stag was lined up in the author's camera lens when companion Frank Elridge scared the animals (and the photographer) by tossing a rock and giving a bloodcurdling yell.

that had to be negotiated in the upper reaches. Anyone who has hunted South Westland knows how well endowed most of the river and creeks are with such obstacles, but I'm sure none has quite as many as the Havelock. There is matted vegetation, moss in abundance and ooze-covered creepers and, seemingly, a lack of birdlife. Ropes and tricounies are essential because it is an area hardly well served with tracks.

Deer sign appeared after Lew and I arrived at the confluence of six streams, a place we named Muchingas which means "place of many gorges". From hereon the ground angled sharply upward and it became impossible to follow the creek which tended to run through a number of narrow waterfalls. Lew and I chose to follow the south face, which seemed the kinder of the two, but even then we were holding on by our fingernails and willpower. The steepness paid a dividend, however. The scrub was finished in one fell swoop and chamois began to appear almost at once. There were no deer in the region, but chamois were everywhere for the taking, and Lew bowled plenty during his trip with a minimum of stalking. Indeed, at the rate he was running through the ammunition I thought he would soon realise the need for caution and begin selecting only potential trophies as targets.

The abundant chamois on the slopes were very quiet, so much so that it was obvious there had been no hunting pressure on the region. On the tops there were simply no deer seen at any time during our expedition, and on slopes that almost shouted "Deer" there was no game. Fodder was plentiful and there seemed no apparent reason why the deer should have neglected the region. The mountain pastures appeared to my eye, at least, to represent deer paradise.

The big drawback in the lack of deer from my own point of view was the need to cook chamois back-steaks in the absence of venison. How I detested the foul-tasting things, but it was a case of like it or lump it until something better turned up for the pot. But there were marvellous compensations. I remember a particular day when we had been walking most of the daylight hours, had found an overhanging rock clear of snow and decided on an early tea with the idea of getting an evening shot or two. While Lew raced around the mountainside, I lay back catching the last rays of sunshine, contentedly puffing a cigarette. Man, it tasted good, especially after those chamois steaks! And as I lay there, I decided it would do me for that day . . . that I would see the sun down from my position from where I could watch the mouth of the Karangarua River flowing into the sea, while by resting the rifle 'scope on my belly I could see clear along to Makawhio Point, a really priceless view.

It was dark when Lew's far cry echoed down to the camp. I lit a piece of car tube (which I used to include in my baggage especially for such occasions) and then set the furiously burning rubber high on a boulder before putting the billy on for a brew. It had been fairly typical of the days we were to spend on the high tops, restful and profitable, the latter because of the easily accessible chamois and their numbers. Lew had a whale of a time. Besides shooting off all his own ammunition, he was able, because we were using the same calibre weapons, to use most of mine as well. However, I was content to let the rascal do all the shooting while I crept around with my camera.

Our trip off the range was by way of a razorback ridge that eventually widened considerably until, towards the lower reaches, it became akin to a fairground railway with its ups and downs, requiring the need to travel by compass which took us out to the road through a knee-deep swamp. Fortunately, our outlet was by a roadman's cottage and we were welcomed with a steaming mug of tea, a gesture much appreciated by two tired hunters.

Looking back, we never actually climbed any particular peak, and our failure to do so is a regret I still harbour. But even if I went back into the region next week I would make sure it was not by that same route up the Havelock. At the time there was no record of the route having been attempted previously, and as far as I know the expedition I took with Lewis Rukavina was a successful first. I sincerely hope it was a pioneering effort, because a couple of weeks after he returned to Christchurch Lew was involved in a serious motor accident which cost him a leg.

George Rawl junior pulled into my driveway at Ross one day and introduced himself as a resident of Beira, Mozambique, where his father operated a prosperous business with the organisation of safaris as a sideline. Young George, as with most "good keen men" with a serious approach to hunting, had a frame covered with just the right amount of flesh and muscle to get by on . . . spare-framed, I think they'd call it in modern fiction. He was fit and he had enjoyed a lot of African hunting on his father's safaris — and had taken a lot of trophies, the latter backed by photographs of him in the field. He had a tight schedule in New Zealand but was hopeful of adding a chamois to his collection.

The Coast weather was far from promising (everything but rain, that is) but we decided to move south and try Mt Adams, which overlooks the Poerua, Barlow and Perth rivers. At that time there was no set track or route on to Mt Adams (7292ft or 2225m) but with the obvious ascent spur leaving the south bank of the Poerua just below the impassable gorge, there was no undue hardship in forcing a passage through the mat of forest to the open snow. Chamois were not really numerous on Mt Adams, but the population was fairly stable - this was before helicopter shooting really got going on chamois — and game was usually available to the keen hunter. The climb in was a far cry from the usual safari travel George was accustomed to in East Africa, but he took it in his stride — literally — and never offered a word of complaint. And he was a capable fellow on the hunt, too. The Coast turned on some magnificent weather, and with its matchless natural beauty the area took a heavy toll of George Rawl's film footage. In return he was able to use his magnificently-finished 7mm magnum to bring down six rather good male chamois, the largest just a whisker under 10½ inches (266.7mm) in horn length. However the trophy was useless because of severe deterioration of one of the bases, and the pelts were not acceptable due to the time of the year.

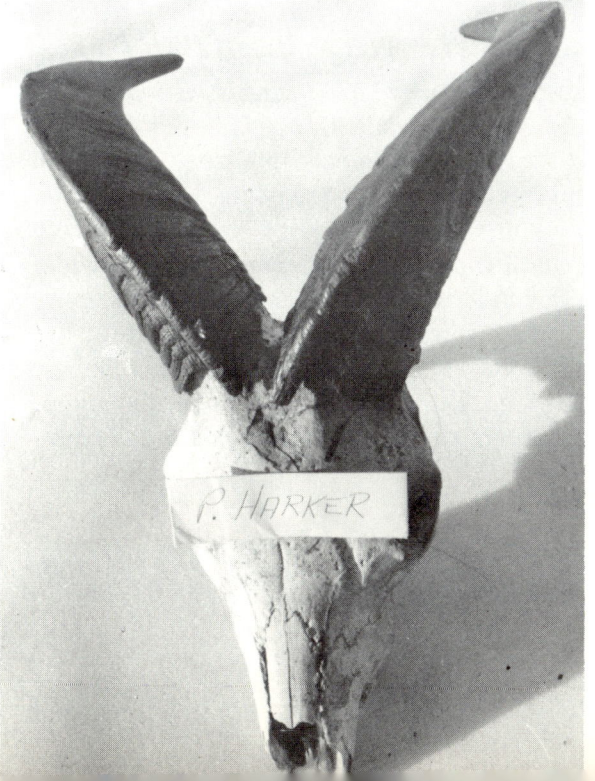
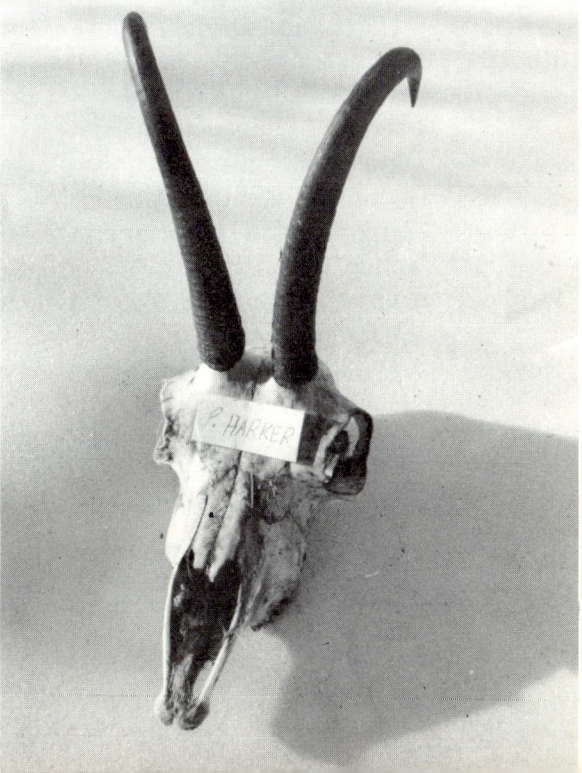

All the trophies did not fall to visitors. The tahr shown has a Douglas score of 46 while the chamois scores 30. The tahr was shot at the head of the Landsborough and the Chamois was shot at the head of Architects Creek.

However, we left the mountain bathed in the reddening amber of the late afternoon sun and made our way down to the terrace, and then on to the grassflats of Keith McKenzie's farm. Yet the day's excitement was not quite finished. We were so engrossed in recounting our various and varied hunting experiences — he in Africa, me in New Zealand — that I did not remember to dry out the car brakes after travelling through a watercourse, and this caused us to shoot off the road into a gorse patch when I braked at the next sharp corner. This experience called for a stop at the Hari Hari Hotel for shock treatment which seemed to be much the same here as in Beira!

It was a pleasure to bypass the last turbulent waterfall and worm our way through the final patch of alpine scrub after the steep climb up Cascade Creek. Bent almost double and, at times, flat on our stomachs pushing our packs ahead of us, we gained finally the open snow tussocks of Mt Trent. I was hunting for four days with Frank Elridge (Auckland), and the difficulties of getting into the region suggested that we would have it to ourselves, despite the fact that it was a four-day holiday weekend. We had studied aerial photographs of the region before going in, and decided it might be better to stay clear of the spurs which appeared to be interlaced with bluffs, and to have a go at negotiating Cascade Creek which seemed to be free of gorges. After a couple of hours from the time we left the riverflats and made our way up the creekbed it seemed the decision had been the correct one. Near the upper reaches, and in view of patches of open tops, we encountered the first of a series of waterfalls, each one proving just that much more difficult to negotiate than the one before it. Yet we were making grand time until we struck the final waterfall. This one stopped us dead in our tracks. It was obvious we would have to backtrack quite a way to find a portion of creek bank which would enable us to make a passage up through the bush, and this we managed eventually to do.

There were already sightings of chamois and quite numerous deer; we quickly established camp and prepared a hot meal so that we could get into the stalking business that very evening. Frank was the first stalker I had been out with who was a dedicated "peep-sight" shooter, and I was keen to see him perform.

The opportunity was quick in coming. We had moved a bare hundred yards from our camp when we sighted a young hind feeding on the edge of the alpine scrub. Frank crawled in the best army commando style into tussock to obtain a good resting shot, and the crack of his 7mm shattered that still evening air and bowled the hind in fine style. The animal had a fine pelt, with the thickest and softest coat any hunter could expect to find, so we took it back to the camp immediately.

While Frank toted the 7mm I was armed with camera and film, and my chance came when we almost ran into a young spiker. He was totally unconcerned about us, to outward appearances, other than cantering away a few feet and then turning to stare intently at us. He'd obviously had no experience with helicopters! So while Frank stood out and engaged the spiker's attention, I crept close towards the animal, using the cover of a rock fault. Indeed, when I poked my telephoto lens over

Less impressive, but still a good head, from a region where tahr were not numerous (head of the Waitaha). This bull sports 13¾ inch (349.25 mm) horns.

The first animal shot in New Zealand with a single-point sight was this large stag, which the author took in the Otoko Valley early in 1969.

Two successful American hunters were Gene Bush, whose tahr measured 13¾ in (349.25 mm), and Bill Sands, who took a 11¼ in (285.75 mm) chamois. Both animals were shot in the Butler River.

the final ridge of rock I almost tapped the spiker on the head. The occasion was a surprise to us both, so I managed only one shot with the camera before the young fellow skipped away.

It was soon afterwards that we came upon a female chamois sunning herself on a tussock ledge, or ridge, overlooking the basin housing the headwaters of the Cascade Creek. The problem was either to take a shot at the chamois and risk spoiling better game opportunities, or to endeavour to sneak by the sentry. We decided to creep into the basin, a decision which gave me a fine photograph of the chamois, and Frank his opportunity to shoot a fine 10-pointer stag. But it was false fortune really, for the weather turned nasty and the gale that night threatened to blow us off the mountainside. It rained and blew, and blew and rained, and there was nothing to do but shelter in our pup tents until the weather passed twenty four hours later.

The wait was worth it, or perhaps it just made the next day seem so much better than it actually was. Anyway, it was a cracking day for stalking, warm and pleasant, and the conditions made the game relax. Frank and I counted thirty seven deer, mostly hinds, and eleven chamois, also mostly females, resting or sleeping. And we also came across a large 8-pointer stag tucked down in the shade of some tall snowgrass, an ideal subject for a photograph. With Frank covering me I crept, then wriggled my way down the mountainside armed with camera and sufficient film to shoot an epic. As I got closer and then closer, my thoughts turned back to an occasion on Mt Allen when I had stalked a little too close to my quarry and had been forced to take to my heels. As I lined the big fellow up in the lens he looked nasty to tangle with, so I was as prepared to run as I was to click the shutter -- and just as well.

Through the camera I saw the stag's head jerk up to coincide with the noise of a thrown rock landing and a bellow of bloodcurdling dimensions from behind me. Shock as much as anything else snapped my finger on the shutter, and the deer could hardly have moved more quickly than I did in bounding away as fast as my legs, working like pistons, would carry me. I have no idea where the stag went, but that prank so angered me that I wanted to reshape Frank's features with my fists until I simmered down and saw the funny side of it. And, as it happened, I got a fine study of a startled stag. What a pity deer don't carry cameras, or that stag would have had an even finer study of a startled Harker!

Roger Fenelk (Sydney), had hunted all New Zealand species of deer and had shot in almost every province of the country when we went out after chamois in 1971. He had previously attempted chamois only once in the Mount Cook region, but bad weather and the shooting pressure of too many hunting parties had ruined his opportunities. We began at dawn, wading into the ice-cold Wanganui River on our way to the Mirage Knob by way of Jones Flat, which lies to the north bank of the Wanganui and Lambert rivers' confluence. The trail, though overgrown, followed a

Cooking out always appeals to visitors on safari. This picture was taken at the confluence of Regina Creek and the Karangarua.

winding ridge up on to the steep snowgrass faces. Though this route actually means going quite a long way up the river, it is certainly the quickest access.

Our first ford was opposite Hot Springs Flat, and though the water was only knee-deep, it was chilly enough to take our breath away. At the next river crossing, at the Hendes Creek confluence, the water was waist-high, and by the time we had scrambled on to the north bank our teeth were chattering. Crossing glacier-fed rivers before the sun had been given time to take some of the chill away really sorted the men from the lads. But we were able to move briskly across a bed of gravel on to an open grassflat which allowed us to proceed at a fairly rapid clip, and to work the cold out of our bones on our way to Jones Flat.

We climbed through the tangle of bush and then the mess of alpine scrub until ten o'clock, when we broke clear and had an unhampered route to the skyline where, in frosty sharpness, the sky stretched in an unbroken vault of blue from the snow-capped mountain tops to the rim of the Tasman Sea. It was one of those sights which occasionally set men to thinking; it was certainly one of the reasons why men climb with or without rifle into the high country.

We climbed towards the top ridge and five chamois bounded from behind a narrow ledge formed by boulders and took off for some distance before stopping to look back and see what the human interlopers were about. Roger had a new rifle, and he soon showed just how effective he could be with it when he lined up on the nearest buck, about 150 yards away. The crack of the rifle and the pitching forward of the chamois seemed to coincide, and Roger managed a second shot (and a second chamois buck) before the group dispersed and disappeared. We skinned both animals and took half an hour to walk on to the west face of Mirage Knob, which looks along the length of the rolling Terriquin Tops. There was an abundance of animal sign and we had counted more than twenty chamois which would have taken little stalking.

Glaciers were sure-fire attractions to most overseas visitors and we used the turbojet helicopter for easy access. This is on the Balfour Glacier, and the odd stance was caused by the slippery ice surface and the author's lack of crampons.

Peter Harker did not take visitors climbing up the Gunn River in this area, but he and his companions went through the centre divide during a period of settled weather for the sheer pleasure of the trip.

We kept to a constant height as we moved through broken moraine fields, stopping occasionally to look for deer on the grass slopes, dotted with huge boulders, along the bushline. But finally we spotted three hinds and a young stag, feeding near the edge of a dry shingle wash, which required little stalking ability. However, Roger was a patient companion as I moved in closer to get some photographs. Once accomplished, the game was open to Roger's rifle and he downed the stag. I had been lying behind a boulder and there seemed to be a lot of lead flying, but perhaps it was merely the echo! Although only a 7-pointer the antlers of the stag were unusual in that they curved inwards to such an extent that the tops were almost touching. I bowled a chamois soon afterwards, being unable to resist a reasonably close-range shot, and Roger gained another. Obviously this was one trip on which we did not have to work hard for our animals. I was delighted that the first male chamois Roger had shot turned out to be a big one: the head later measured out at 10¾ in. (273.05mm) with a wide spread and thick base.

But the day was to provide even better luck. I later shot a buck chamois which looked average enough from a distance, yet carried horns with a measurement of 11¼ins (285.75mm), my second-best that year.

It was while working on this animal that I noticed Roger had a swollen knee he kept rubbing, and as I took greater notice I discovered that he not only limped, but winced with each step. Not a word from him about it, so I suggested that we had enjoyed a pretty wonderful day's shooting and it might be a good time to make our way back in leisurely manner, rather than go on. It was a wise decision, because his knee got steadily worse and it became a case of "Sherpa" Harker tottering along the final mile or two loaded with everything including the kitchen sink. It was probably this factor which later caused me to miss my step by the river, fall in and lose the only torch we had.

A letter later received from Roger told how he spent some time in hospital having a cartilage removed — and of his determination to return to Mirage Knob after the easy shooting. I was in there later, but the helicopters on commercial meat-recovery had also been there and the days of easy shooting were all in the past tense.

Paul Olsen and his wife were in New Zealand in 1972 on a hunting and fishing holiday, and I was asked to act as their guide on a safari which we agreed should take in the head of the Landsborough River for tahr, the Douglas River for red deer, and a high, hanging basin on the south side of the top portion of Architect's Creek as the most likely spot for trophy-standard chamois. Goodwin McNutt flew us over the pass from the Cook River to Architect's Creek, and let the helicopter idle slowly down and into the hanging basin. We were down almost to auto-rotation as we crept through the opening and over the open snow tussock where several female chamois burst from cover and led their kids scampering away in front of the whirling 'copter blades.

A fine buck chamois came bounding down a shingle fan and stood watching for our next move as McNutt reversed the helicopter and moved back around the mountainside out of sight of the game. We landed, and while McNutt flew Mrs Olsen off to view the scenery, Paul and I climbed higher, taking care not to dislodge shale or make any other noise likely to scare the game. Stalking chamois after the departure of a helicopter, as in this particular case, provided problems for the hunters because the animals became extremely cautious and alert for any sound. We parked ourselves behind a boulder which, if the landmarks I had taken earlier were correct and the animal had not moved too far, should have placed us about sixty yards from the buck.

I indicated by gesture to Paul to regain his breath from the climb, then to put a bullet into the breech of his rifle and leave the bolt open. Slowly we crawled around the boulder to peer across the slip. Nothing stirred. Paul was so eager that he had stood upright before I could stop him, and there was a rattle of rock slightly above us as the chamois catapulted out of a shallow depression in the shale. At full gallop he appeared to cover the ground without touching the surface, a wonderful sight of grace and motion. When he reached the far side of the slip he braked, and turned to look back at us. Paul rested his rifle on a boulder and took a hurried sight. The shot was a good one, and the chamois tumbled forward.

It produced horns of trophy standard, and with a fine pelt in winter colours the first victim of the hunt had given the safari a wonderful beginning.

We were collected by the helicopter and flew across the tops into the headwaters of the Landsborough River, where we found about eight mobs of tahr, perhaps as many as fifty animals altogether, all nannies with their young. It took some ten minutes to locate any bull tahr, and we discovered these well down the valley, living in the alpine scrub. Once again we were dropped from the helicopter, and went after a group of seven bulls.

The alpine scrub caused us some problems, but we eventually managed to get up to a commanding position, above a bull tahr moving through the bush towards a clear piece of ground he would have to cross if he maintained his line. The wait was brief, and the tahr was dead by the time he hit the ground.

Two shots, two species. It seemed too good to be true, so I bet Paul Olsen he could not make three species with three shots. He had the tahr and the chamois; he needed a red deer.

The trophy tahr measured more than 13 inches (330.2mm) and gained a lot of points for the thickness around the base of the horns, a very fine trophy animal indeed. The Olsens would not believe me when I told them the bull would weigh more than 130 pounds, but after they tried to roll it over and then to lift the front portion of the carcase, they were satisfied with my estimate.

Paul, his wife and I decided to stay overnight in the Douglas hut, so we sent the helicopter back to Fox Glacier with instructions to collect us the next day. We walked down river, angled up to a high lip overlooking the tail of the Horace Walker Glacier and took a rest on the first portion of even ground we struck. It was from here that I noticed three deer watching us from a marshy depression in the valley

The author was sitting behind a rock pile when this chamois bounded by, and he shot it with the rifle between his knees without even the need to aim.

below us. I told Paul to watch the deer and me carefully, but not to fire until I waved to him. Paul was left sitting in full view of the deer to hold their attention while I slipped over the rim of the spur and went around the steep shale slope out of sight of the valley. This track brought me to the side of the deer, but within sight of Paul. Selecting a nice flat stone I skimmed it towards the scrub behind the deer. As it landed, the deer bounded forward into the open and I waved to Paul. I saw the rifle go to his shoulder, and then saw the deer stumble as the shot boomed. We each walked down the slope until our paths crossed, and then began a search through the bracken and shoulder-high snow tussock until we found the carcase.

    I had lost the bet, and that night was to serve as sole cook, waiter, dishwasher and suppermaker as penalty. However, after our meal a jubilant Paul Olsen produced a huge bottle of Scotch which seriously delayed the normal household chores and produced next morning two bleary-eyed hunters who needed the brisk walk to the Douglas Lake to rekindle health and vigour. By the time the helicopter swooped in to pick us up and carry back Paul's three-shot trophies, sore heads were of no account.

    That safari was to have far-reaching effects on the lives of my family and myself. Paul Olsen operated a sportswear manufacturing complex back in Michigan, and he offered me the opportunity to join his organisation. There was an impressive salary, a contract that ensured security, and the kindness of Mrs Olsen in writing to my wife with information about housing, schools, and the multifarious things women must know about before they'll budge with a family. It was an attractive proposition and at one stage my wife Julie and I decided that we would go to the United States.

    It was a big step, and it was one reason I took the opportunity of accompanying Don Finlayson and "Doc" Rudumsky, of Hokitika, on a helicopter trip to Stewart Island to fly bridge-building and hut materials in for the Forest Service. This break away from Ross and the Coast gave me time to get my thinking into some sort of order. It also gave my wife an opportunity to settle her own ideas without my influence. After the Stewart Island excursion, I had a longish trip organised into the Maitahi and Perth River regions with Bruce Wright and George Lindsay, and by the time I returned to Ross the decision was made: both my wife and myself agreed that it would be to the advantage of the children to stay in New Zealand.

But the soul-searching we went through then made it clear to me that my days as a hunter were about finished. The years were slipping by — happily it was true — but there was an increase in the aches and pains that arrived with the colder weather, and my ability to clamber over the high country I loved so much would become increasingly limited. Not only that, the continual game-killing had robbed high country ventures of their attraction. The time for decision had come, sparked off by that safari with Paul Olsen, and it has led me to Otago as Manager-Secretary of the Otago Acclimatisation Society.

CHAPTER ELEVEN

RETROSPECT

SOUTHERN WESTLAND has more characters to the acre than any region I know. It was my pleasure to meet and talk with many of them, and to hunt with a few of them. They were, in the main, men of a type: independent and free-spirited with a deep love of the mountains and valleys where they would live, like the game they hunted, for weeks or months at a time without companions, without food other than a few basics, and without contact of any kind with civilisation.

But the remote regions of the West Coast have not remained free from technological advance. The Man-Alone figure of even a few years ago has virtually gone, even from Southern Westland. Its rugged peaks, matted scrub and forests and vast shingleflats have been made so easily accessible by aircraft and helicopter that there are few places remaining which cannot be hunted by those with the stamina and determination to do so. There are today fewer and fewer of the hermitlike figures who used to reappear from their remote blocks every several months for a mighty and memorable celebration and then disappear again to be seldom reported until the next one.

The helicopter has changed the hunting patterns just as surely as it has changed the distribution of game throughout the region. The fact that 50,000 or more game animals have continued to be taken out of Southern Westland year after year emphasises the density that existed of these intensive-grazing animals — and the need there has been drastically to reduce those numbers. Even today there is no definitive evidence that the deer, chamois and tahr populations have been brought under control, despite the heavy inroads made by commercial meat-hunting and the fact that the helicopter shooter has to work so much harder now to get economic tallies.

Many of the men who used to shoot the area have dropped out of the game meat industry, but they remain on the Coast because they are as much a part of the region as it is of them. Westland is like the mistress to whom even the happily married man must occasionally return.

During my seven years there, based at Ross, I had the experience of seeing my home become a staging place for Good Keen Men eager to try their skills in the most rugged hunting country New Zealand has to offer. This was due largely to the weekly articles which appeared in the *Christchurch Star Sports*, and to a lesser extent to pieces I wrote for magazines in other countries, as well as word-of-mouth

"The Man-Alone figure has virtually gone..." The helicopter has brought the most inaccessible places within reach of everyone.

information that I could offer advice on the best areas for those long on desire for trophies or pelts, but short on time.

In deciding to give it all away, I was giving up people as much as places, and a way of life that was immensely satisfying, even when it was not always financially rewarding. Everyone likes to feel that they have left something worthwhile as they have passed along, and my real rewards were in sharing the country with others . . . in the miles of tracks I helped to cut or blaze . . . the contribution I was able to make to remapping the region . . . the pleasure of those I was able to lead into new areas which gave them their trophies.

Even away from the Coast, my experiences there are a continuing source of pleasure. I have the excellent fortune of being able to run through my mind like an old movie hundreds of expeditions, safaris and trips which took me up all the rivers, valley and passes (except Gap Pass up the Landsborough) along the whole of the Western Alps. This wonderful sense of recall is backed by a file of photographs and colour slides that is numbered in thousands rather than hundreds, and when I look at them I can see the sun caressing the snow-cloaked peaks, the kaleidoscope of early morning and late evening colours . . . hear the shrill whistle of the chamois or tahr on the higher reaches, or the roar of the red stag challenging his rivals . . . .

Sometimes I can smell the sickly taint of turbo-jet kerosene or av-gas as keenly as the more pleasant and pungent odour of woodsmoke from a campfire.

Like the child who never grew up, I can still get a thrill from the *whoomp* of a helicopter jet, even while I have no desire to get back on the step and test the firmness of hand and keenness of eye essential to down game from an aerial platform.

I miss the laughter and stories and discussions which seemed so much funnier or serious, depending on the circumstances, when they occurred in the light of a guttering candle with West Coast rain pounding on to the corrugated iron roof of a remote hut in the mountains, and a river raging by.

Rutting deer in the head of the Edison photographed during the author's last major three-month safari with Barry Petrie.

Increasingly, the author's camera took precedence over his rifle, and this animal caught napping by Pollock Creek was able to escape.

Alan Weir and his young companion show off some impressive velvet.

A young hind... so attractive, yet so destructive.

It is easier to be your own man on the Coast, where values are different and a bloke is judged for what he is and not for what he has, or has not, got. A good argument can be made that the hunting life is limiting, that it offers no new horizons and few challenges to the professional, and that that is why so few remain dedicated to it.

Yet as I flip through my diary for 1971 I see that in January I had an expedition to the head of the Karangarua, and in February another to the head of the Kensington. March saw the beginning of a three-month safari with Barry Petrie which took us to the Edison River, the Waitoto, Casey's Creek, the Drake and Donald, plus high points along the Haast Range. We did this on foot, while by helicopter we visited the Troyte, Regina, Douglas, Horace Walker, Architect's, Balfour, Cook, Jacob's, Lambert, Adams and others. We went by fixed-wing plane to the Upper Cascade and Landsborough.

In June there was an exploration to the upper part of the Perth, a trip by car to Ikamatua where we spent some time on the tops hunting fallow deer before heading south to hunt chamois at Scamper Torrent.

The second part of the year began with live-game capture in the Gunn and Whataroa River regions, while in August there was helicopter work and a trip to the Upper Clarke River area with Allan Fairhall. September brought a journey through Robinson's Gorge to the open tussock slopes between Mt Hitchen and Mt Allen, while October brought a shooting trip with Roger Fenelk to Mirage Knob. I spent a lot of November shooting and laughing with Ernie Wilson and then moved up the Edison for some pre-Christmas work.

Harry Hawker used to shoot the Arawata and Jackson Rivers, and also operated jetboats in the region.

Tom Paris, an early companion who subsequently left the Coast, in the lower rim of the basin at the head of the Little Waitaha. Back in the late 1960s this area provided deer and chamois which were numbered in dozens.

Joe Crawford (*left*) and Dave Barton (*right*) were meat-hunting characters in the Cascade Valley region.

A trophy-class chamois in the Karangarua Valley.

During this time I was preparing a regular weekly article for publication in Christchurch, and I must pay tribute to those numerous hunters, trampers and pilots whose cooperation and kindness ensured that my deadlines were always met. I remember once flagging down a helicopter early one morning while I was still in my underpants. The pilot, the late Tony Hawker, was a wonderful fellow and one of the characters of the Coast, and he promised not only to take my article, but to see that it was posted at Haast that day: an airmail service from the back of beyond! But there were other pilots of planes and helicopters — once, even, a chap on a horse who promised to get it to a postbox within three or four days, and did so. Buffalo Bill had nothing on those Coasters.

But it had to end. I could be there yet, I suppose, doing much the same things as I did in 1971. But the fact that I was able to make the decision in 1972 to leave was the result of an amalgam of reasons which didn't become clear to me until I was away from the region and settled in the new job in Dunedin.

The love of the mountains remained, but the need for a more settled existence to provide a stable environment for my children had proven a stronger desire. My friends and companions of those hunting years have, like me, opted to follow new paths. Barry Petrie is with the Catchment Board in North Westland, Peter Billington has an engineering and architectural business at Rangiora, while Paul Bevernage is second engineer on a cargo ship. Ernie Wilson has gone crayfishing in the Deep South, but Alan Weir remained true to his trade and at last sighting was shooting from helicopters for Alpine.

The majority of the meat-hunters who operated jetboats or horses, planes or helicopters, or simply tramped the area and got their game out as best they might, have found the hygiene regulations so tough and the price of game meat so low that most of them have pulled out of their blocks and left them to the company helicopters. Ron Hogland, who used to shoot the Lower Paringa and Doughboy Creek, now operates the motor camp at Paringa; Jack Condon, who shot the Maitahi and Pannel Creek, has a fishing boat; Tony Condon, who operated in the Paringa and Otoka, is now back farming at Paringa.

Harry Hawker is engaged in maintenance work for a large contracting outfit at Haast today, but he used to shoot the Arawata region, and for a time operated jetboats until a series of accidents wiped them off. The Westland rivers proved difficult even for jetboats to conquer. Cliff Peart, who did so much good work in the Upper Waitoto, is a carpenter at Haast township, but Grahame Allan, who began as a foot shooter and moved on to aircraft, now pilots a helicopter for Alpine.

The fliers have remained faithful to the region, for it is one with special problems, requiring special knowledge and skills. Typical of these men are Howard Smith, who earned his own aircraft by shearing and contracting and now flies helicopters for a North Island company, and Jim Wilson, who pilots helicopters but has as well mechanical skills which are at a premium in the sort of meat-recovery work in which he is engaged. And there is Goodwin McNutt, who was a pioneer in the use of aircraft for meat recovery, operating still from Fox Glacier but concentrating today on tourist and general flying work with his jet helicopter.

These are the sort of men it was a pleasure to know and to work with during my own years up and down the South Westland region. They are still there, and I can, and do, go back to see them occasionally. But increasingly I realise that the general cast of characters involved in meat-recovery and hunting has changed drastically since I was a part of the action. Each year away from it widens the gap that separates me from the industry and the sport today.

But I still have a storehouse of memories of people and places that is irreplaceable. I can look back without regret because I was able to do what I did in South Westland . . . to test myself against the challenges of mountain and river while in my physical prime. And if I want to go back to try again, certainly at a more sedate pace, the opportunity remains.

People may change, but the mountains hardly change at all . . .

APPENDIX

HANDY HARKER HINTS

IT IS POSSIBLE to provide acres of information on the "right" sort of gear with which to go hunting, but this won't really help to put the trophy head on your wall or the beautiful skin on your floor. Those who go into the hills require a weapon suitable for the game they intend to hunt, a sharp knife, and sensible clothes for the type of conditions they intend to meet and the length of time to be spent there. The higher the hunting ground, the warmer the clothing, the stronger the boots, the greater the need for sustaining food and for proper shelter.

Basically, the man who intends to go hunting must use his common sense. He should get as much reliable information as possible from official sources about hut accommodation, tracks, weather conditions and the like when he begins planning. Some readers might read in an occasional experience reported in these pages that I tended to undertake the odd expeditions without the careful planning I am suggesting here, and this would be quite true. But the area in which I operated was country I had learned about from firsthand experience, by walking up its river and ridges, skirting its lakes and glaciers, climbing its mountains, and cutting my own tracks where necessary.

Thus, the clothing required for hunting tahr at over 5,000 feet (1500 metres) is not what is worn when stalking red deer in the lowlands. If you want to go after the big tahr on the highest ice and snowfields of South Westland, usually in the range between 5,000 and 6,000ft (1500-1800 metres), then you need to be concerned about more than the right gear to wear. Even when shooting from helicopters in midwinter at these altitudes it was difficult to retrieve animals, so the hunter on foot should know what is in store for him.

If he wants to have a go, I would suggest *crampons* of the grivel lobster-claw type with quick-release straps. Those with twelve points are better than those with ten points.

For hunting, the short shaft *ice axe* is best as it can be fitted to slots alongside the frame pack for easy travel into the valley heads. From my experience I would suggest the MacInnes hiduminium shafted axe as the very best for climbing steep faces because of its ease of management. An ice axe has many uses, and hunters should put in some swot before setting out for country in which this most useful tool is necessary.

Similarly with ropes only the best is good enough. Nylon is preferred and there

An overhanging rock is better than an expensive tent in providing safe shelter. This one, occupied by Bruce Wright, is in the head of the Otoko Valley.

should be at least 30 yards of it, but I strongly advise that, despite its strength and flexibility, it be closely inspected before every trip, and also that it be replaced after five or six trips. There is a tendency for it to fray on rocky terrain, and its cheapness enables early replacement.

In all seriousness, let me suggest now that every high climbing hunter should carry a pair of *old woollen socks* which might be a lifesaver in the event of encountering wet and greasy rocks. Just slip the socks over the boots and tie them in place with string. Sometimes snowfields are divided by a ridge of steepish rock, and it takes just a couple of minutes to slip the old socks over the boots. When not required over the boots, they can be used as gloves!

Hunting at heights over 5,000 ft (1500 metres) really is a serious proposition and should not be undertaken by anyone without extensive experience, and this is best gained by being with parties which have it. Having the right equipment is one aspect of the issue; *knowing your own capabilities* is much more important. The good hunter can usually judge from previous experience whether he can cross an icefield or follow a sharp razorback ridge. When he feels he cannot do it he backs off and seeks another route. It is the inexperienced and the overconfident who commit themselves beyond their capabilities.

Hunters are not supposed to be mountaineers, so if there is a fear or even a dislike of heights then the hunter should seek his tahr in the slips and creeks in the upper valleys, rather than try the tops. I can speak with some authority about the foolishness of commitment beyond experience at height while chasing tahr, because I made some of my own mistakes there and was fortunate to escape without injury. One of these occasions involved Bruce Wright and George Lindsay as my companions, crossing an icefield in the Upper Perth Valley. The crossing involved a traverse of a 45-degree angled icefield. Below was a thousand feet of nothing; above several hundred feet of soft snow over ice. We were not prepared for these conditions, because we had not originally planned to hunt so high, so we had neither rope nor ice axes, and were chipping footholds in the ice with Bruce's rifle.

These pictures were taken within ten hours of each other — the Maitahi sparkling between high boulders (*top*) and heavily in flood and impassable with trees and debris being swept by.

Boulder-hopping is an essential skill in South Westland. Barry Petrie gives a demonstration here in the Upper Perth Valley. Debris high on the banks suggests the water has at times risen eighteen feet.

We were perched halfway across the ice barrier when the snow about us began to move. Several large areas broke away and swirled around and past us, but did not sweep us along with it fortunately. And then the remaining snow seemed to stabilise, so we managed to complete our crossing and thank our lucky stars for a fortune we really did not deserve.

It is, however, easy to admit foolishness once it has occurred without tragic results. The true test is to learn one's capabilities and stay within them. The hunter who can do that should strike a minimum of trouble and gain a maximum of pleasure from his sport and/or job.

The time to learn about "idiot acts" is around the campfire when stories are told to while away the hours, and though some of them tend to get a gilding with each re-telling there is nonetheless the core of truthful experience remaining. I remember when Alan Weir, Neil Connely and I were at the head of Gunn Creek in the middle of winter at about 4,500ft (1400 metres) when a number of tahr were seen on a narrow ridge above us. Alan decided to clamber up behind the animals to cut off their line of retreat, while Neil and I scaled around an icefield below them to prevent the wily tahr from descending. On this particular occasion we had a rope with us, and we used it to cross the ice. All the way across the ice cracked and groaned whenever we moved.

At the end of the ridge we spotted Alan on a high rock pillar, and it seemed that something was amiss. We stared up until the shock realisation came to us that the snow and ice below him had slipped away and he was trapped. This required that I should straddle the ridge, like on a horse, and work my way towards him so that the rope could be twirled cowboy-fashion up to him from a sitting position. "Heigh-yo Silver" had nothing on me as the thin winter wind cut through my clothing, and my hands became less and less flexible with each attempt to toss him the rope. When he did catch a lucky throw he was able to loop the rope over a rock outcrop and lower himself towards my position on the ridge. Without that rope we would have been in all manner of trouble, and would certainly have had to contemplate a night out in conditions well below freezing.

It is easy to preach right from wrong in mountain behaviour from the comfort of a warm room, yet it is easier still to overlook obvious preparations which every hunter who seeks game at high altitudes should make. For instance, everyone going after tahr and chamois in ice or snow conditions should know how to stop themselves from a long and dangerous fall, always on the cards when operating in steep, hard snow conditions. Hunters must learn to react immediately they begin to slip, or their slide may gain so much momentum that there will be little chance of applying the brakes. As soon as a mis-step occurs and the hunter begins to fall, he must roll to face the snow and plunge the blade of his ice axe into the surface (use the spike if possible) while keeping the toes of his boots pressed against the surface as strongly as possible. A prayer is never out of place in these circumstances, either.

The possibility of being caught out at high altitudes in winter conditions requir-

This is the camp we "lived in" while hunting the Upper Cascade Valley. We were continually wet for days on end and when the weather did clear for short spells the sandflies and mosquitoes were around in black clouds.

ing a night on the mountain should always be planned for in high altitude hunting. True, the average hunter should be fairly close to the alpine fringe so he should make for this region to find a niche in which to establish himself. Plenty of bracken heaped over a rock or convenient scrub can make a comfortable if cold bed.

However, the party caught in snow without opportunity to get into alpine scrub should know how to go about making a *snow cave*. First, give thoughts of making an igloo a miss. Working with schoolroom materials the task seems easy enough, but in the reality of winter conditions on a mountainside it is not on for any but the most skilful. Igloos usually collapse, but quite apart from their building difficulties they consume too much time and energy, particularly the latter. I favour leaving igloos to the Eskimos. A snow cave is much easier to provide, but let me emphasise as strongly as possible that the use of it should be a last resort, adopted only if the party cannot make it back to the bush edge.

In my experience it takes about two hours of solid slog to dig a snow cave or build up snow beside a leaning rock to cavelike proportions. If the cave is built wholly of snow it is necessary to find a snowbank at an angle of about 30 or 35 degrees. These are usually found by a rock abutment or a stream bank. Once deciding the site, use the ice axe to break up the inside snow and stamp it with crampons still attached. Start several feet apart, working the cave into the shape of a letter T, and making sure the entrance is lower than the cave itself. This ensures that air warmed by the body is retained in the cave. From inside the finished structure it is possible partially to block the entrance with snow, or even packs. Always retain at least one ice axe inside in case of a collapse, and remember a properly hammered out snow cave can be a lifesaver.

Heading up the Otoko, showing obstacles and the ruggedness encountered in this terrain.

Fog conditions can be another curse for hunters operating above 4,000 feet on the Coast, especially as high bluffs and deep gorges are very numerous. I class the conditions in two categories: (1) fog which allows a restricted visibility of up to thirty yards and (2) whiteout conditions where visibility is restricted to about four yards. Even following game trails can result in the hunter's arrival at the edge of a sudden "drop-off", for while tahr and chamois can scramble down the face of a cliff, the hunter laden with pack and rifle does not have the same facility. Worse, unless he moves with the greatest care he can walk over a forty or sixty foot drop. So it is essential in fog to keep a sharp lookout for any sort of landmark or sign — even a boot print — to provide clues on direction. In a whiteout there is only one thing to do: sit tight, make a nest in the tussock or alpine scrub (or, if need be, a snow cave) and wait it out. The essential thing is to keep busy and avoid panic. Whiteouts prove the old saw that patience is a virtue.

In any event, restricted vision tends to distort the appearance of familiar surroundings . . . the sounds of rivers or creeks are muffled or amplified, and it is possible to become the victim of your imagination. In bad visibility I found the most satisfactory method for travelling in snow-covered terrain that varied from soft-powdered snow to a hard-packed icy surface was to use a salt-shaker. It was my insurance against getting lost. I would grind up Condy's Crystals to a fine texture and fill a large plastic salt-shaker with them. Once I hit the hard snow and ice I would sprinkle the Condy's on to the surface; one shake would produce a brilliant purple circle about fifteen inches in diameter. The shake would be repeated at every 100 steps except in soft snow, where my footprints left a sufficient marker, so if I struck fog or a whiteout I had little difficulty retracing my steps. And I have

Whiteout on the way! Bruce Slater at the head of Dry Creek, 100 feet above Scone Basin, during adverse weather conditions. Five minutes after taking this photograph visibility dropped to less than ten feet.

Basil Detloft thigh-deep in snow on Mt Allen.

Barry Petrie with a deer, carried to give him freedom to use his rifle should he encounter another deer on his way back to camp.

quite distinct recollections of occasions when those purple splotches on the snow kept me safely on the right track during a homeward journey.

With *bush travel*, problems are most usually encountered during the descent from the tops to the valley floor. While there is little difficulty in following a creek into the mountains and then catching a spur and following it through to the top, the descent is not always as easy. All spurs seem to be the same.

My method to overcome this problem should have been patented, but I never quite got around to it. I used a roll of toilet paper. My usual method was to use coloured toilet paper; the roll dropped over my rifle barrel rotated well enough to enable me to tear off a strip every fifty yards or so and spike it on a piece of scrub or over a jagged stick or rock. It was usually possible to leave the "marker" without even breaking stride. In my experience a toilet roll should last the length of most West Coast spurs, and the advantage was there plain to see on the return journey. The other advantage of the system was that it did not remain to confuse later hunting parties, for the soft paper usually disintegrated within a week.

It is very easy to get lost hunting on the Coast. Much of the area is heavily bushed, yet even after straying, hunting parties should be able to get themselves back on to the homeward track by taking time to consider their circumstances and then using some commonsense. In my view too many of the so-called guidebooks to hunting cause more trouble than they are worth because their information is outdated. It is difficult, except in quickly produced pamphlets or the like, to keep bush, track and game-animal density figures up to date, and most experienced weekend hunters probably make due allowance for some change during the production time of the normal expert book. But there is no excuse for guide information which is years out of date, or which is listed on the say-so of someone other than the author. This is one reason why I have refused here to provide such information.

There is one firm rule for the party which gets lost: sit down, roll a smoke, and try and nut things out. If there is level going in a mid-valley section then it should be obvious that the track follows the easiest route. In most cases this will be along the riverbank. It simply means the party goes to the river edge and follows the stream up until the track is picked up again. No one is going to cut a track around a hillside if there is a flattish bench alongside the river.

However, if the track still eludes you, head out to the riverbed and take a close look at the terrain you have come from. Place yourself then in the track-cutter's position: pick the easiest route, as he would doubtless do. And once a terrace is sighted with steep surroundings you can be sure the track follows the bench.

In upper valley reaches the same principles apply. In valleys where there are no tracks then you cannot get lost. Just press ahead, keeping an eye peeled for game trails to skirt bluffs and narrow gorges. Unfortunately, it is usually the walk out which provides the problems and produces the accidents because hunters have used their energies, perhaps over-used them, stalking game and making the tops. And it is when the group is tired and weary that mistakes are made. A fifteen minute rest and a smoke, perhaps some food, provides the opportunity to relax and

Steep shale country at the head of the Douglas River, where a mis-step is particularly dangerous and ice and rockfalls are common from the towering bluffs overhead.

rethink the situation. It is important in my view that hunting parties have a leader who can set a norm for the group so that the weaker members do not over-stretch themselves to keep up with the stronger members, and end up as a burden on the whole group. A leader who knows the people he is tramping and hunting with, and who particularly knows their capabilities, can add immense enjoyment to an expedition by ensuring that everyone has an opportunity to "do their own thing" within the limits of their strength and abilities.

Everyone who has hunted on the Coast knows that one of the major obstacles involves flood waters. Because of the rapid run-off between the mountains and the short distance through the flatlands, a river can rise by from eight to sixteen feet in as many hours. Side creeks that are usually dry or contain a mere trickle of water can become an uncrossable barrier in a very, very short time. In the main, West Coast hunters do not bother to carry ropes. Except in the higher country, as mentioned above, they are hardly essential. Access by moving up or down West Coast rivers is largely from riverflat to riverflat plus a certain amount of "bush-bashing"; and river crossings for the most part are time-savers.

There is all manner of official information about how to cross rivers, but my advice to hunters is to know when *not* to cross. For instance, those small parties travelling without ropes, or the solo hunter, should never attempt to cross a flooded river or stream when the bottom can be heard moving . . . the sound of stones or boulders being moved by the current. Nor should crossings be made at rapids situated upstream from a bluff, as one slip can result in the hunter being washed down into the deeper water below the bluffs where conflicting currents provide

The head of the Perth, and the sort of bluffs which provide a fall to nowhere.

additional dangers. Never cross swollen waters when trees and branches are being swept past, nor make an attempt in a narrow section when the banks are strewn with boulders. These indicate a rough bottom and the likelihood of deep holes.

Hunters should certainly recognise that when carrying a heavy pack or an animal carcase that it is dangerous to cross any wide stretch of swollen water where the depth cannot be fairly accurately judged, or where the opposite bank is perpendicular. This indicates the deepest flow with the strongest current and, once embarked upon, might mean total commitment. And, finally, swirling, oily-looking flood waters usually encountered in the northern West Coast region should always be treated with respect as the current is very deceptive. If the depth cannot be gauged, then do not attempt a crossing.

And do not roam far from your base camp without food. My own system for enjoying a hot meal in the mountains, without the need to carry the kitchen sink along, was simple and effective. I used to attach my king-sized enamel mug to my knife-belt, and in one shirt pocket went a packet of powdered thick soup powder and a meat extract cube. In the other pocket I put a handful of solid fuel blocks. All these items are small and light, and take a minimum of pocket space. As a smoker, I always had matches, so the non-smoker should remember a firestick!

Thus when the old tummy began to voice an opinion, I used to stop by water and brew up. I used two stones, just slightly thicker than the fuel blocks, and set the mug on these. After lighting the fuel blocks, I closed the open ends of the "hob" with two more stones to retain the heat in the recess, and just waited until the mugful of water became hot enough to drop in the soup or meat extract cube. And with tea bags on the market, a leaf-free brew-up is easy. It used to take two fuel blocks to boil water in my large enamel mug, so the cartage problem was negligible. The advantage of warming soup or tea in the higher reaches made the brew-up almost as important as my cigarette.

How's that for a mixed set of priorities!

OTHER REED BOOKS FOR HUNTERS

HUNTING IN NEW ZEALAND, *by Rex Forrester*, is the standard work on the subject. Most amusingly written, but completely comprehensive and authoritative. Fully illustrated with superb hunting photographs.

THE SHARPSHOOTER, *by Matt and Bruce Grant*, is an invaluable guide for hunters who wish to get optimum performance from their rifles, sights and ammunition. A layman's guide to a scientific subject.

RED STAGS CALLING, *by G.G. Atkinson*. The author is a veteran trophy man who learned his skills from the MacConochie brothers and gained magnificent heads in the Rakaia in the greatest days of that herd.

FIREARMS AND HUNTING, by P.C. Logan and L.H. Harris, is published by Reeds in association with the National Mountain Safety Council. Costing less than a dollar, this guide sums up what every sane hunter must know and do to ensure the safety of himself, his companions, and the public. Required reading for every youngster who acquires a gun or rifle.

A GUIDE TO MODELMAKING AND TAXIDERMY, *by Leo Cappel*, taxidermist at Auckland Museum. A craftbook essential for every hunter who wishes to preserve and mount his own trophies — deer, trout or gamebirds.